D0459102

How to play

Chess

Kevin Wicker

with a foreword by David Pritchard

Illustrated by Karel Feuerstein

TREASURE PRESS

Acknowledgments

The author would like to thank Bob Wade for help with the diagrams and with advice, and also especial thanks are due to Rosemary Hannan for typing out the manuscript.

First published in Great Britain in 1977 by The Hamlyn Publishing Group Limited

This edition published in 1988 by Treasure Press 59 Grosvenor Street London W1

ISBN 1 85051 302 3

Printed by Mandarin Offset in Hong Kong

Contents

Foreword   8
Introduction   9

Chapter One: How to Play   11
How the Men Move   11
Rules   14
The Strengths of the Pieces   15
The Notation   15

Chapter Two: Tactics   17
Combinations   17
Decoy Combinations   18
Combinations to Win Enemy Pieces   20
Combinations Used for Promotion   21
Drawing Combinations   21
Zugzwang   22
Zwischenzug   23
Example Positions   23
Answers   26

Chapter Three: Strategy   27
General Principles   27
Planning   38

Chapter Four: The Phases of the Game   41
The Opening   41
The Endgame   45

Chapter Five: Some Illustrative Games   50

Further Reading   59
Index   60

Foreword

by David Pritchard, Editor
Games & Puzzles

The popularity of chess has grown dramatically in the last decade, and it is now probably the best-known game in the world.

Anyone who has learnt to play does not have to be told why this is so; it is a pleasure which awaits the reader of Kevin Wicker's concise and complete guide.

Chess has the appearance of being complicated. It is not. Thousands of very young children play, and some play it well. It is a game like most other games, indoor or outdoor: the rules are few but mastery is for the few.

This book will not make you a master. What it will do is show you the rules and how they work, explain basic tactics and strategy, and tell you how to start the game, how to conduct the middlegame, which is the main battle, and what to aim for in the endgame. At the end, you should be a competent player, ready, if you so wish, to enter the clamorous world of clubs and congresses and to enjoy the vast library of books on the game.

Chess moves can be recorded, and a knowledge of chess notation is a key which opens a wonderful door. Firstly, there is the literature: all important tournament and match games of the last hundred years, and more, are preserved for study and enjoyment. In very few games is it possible to arrange, at your own place and convenience, an action replay of some memorable battle of the past (or of the present—probably millions of people round the world folowed the famous Fischer-Spassky match in their own homes). And secondly, you will be able to record your own games, to return to them later in pleasure or sorrow, and to measure your improvement.

Both types of notation currently in use are fully explained in this book, and the many illustrations will make the text easy to follow.

Introduction

Chess, the 'Royal Game', is believed to have originated in India in the sixth century A.D. As it spread through Asia, Northern Africa, and Europe, both the rules and the powers of the pieces underwent considerable mutation. The modern rules are described in Chapter One.

The board consists of sixty-four squares, alternately black and white for clarity, and at the start of the game each player has sixteen men set up as shown in Figure 1.

The pieces on the respective back ranks, from left to right, are known as rook, knight, bishop, queen, king, bishop, knight, and rook. Each player has a row of eight pawns

Fig. 1

in front of his pieces. Pawns are not usually referred to as pieces; the collective term for pawns and pieces is 'men'.

Whatever the actual colours of the board squares and the men, both are always termed black and white. The player of the white pieces is referred to as White, and the player of the black pieces, Black.

Referring again to Figure 1, you will see that there is a white square in the right-hand corner nearest each player. Also, the white queen is on a white square and the black queen on a black; apart from king and queen, all the other men are symmetrically

9

placed. The initial position, as it is known, is always set up in this way.

In almost all chess illustrations White is shown playing up the board. This is because White has the advantage of the first move, after which both sides move alternately.

The first move in chess confers an advantage on White for two reasons: firstly, chess is a fast-moving game, and an extra active piece often helps to turn the tide of battle. The tactical strengths of the various pieces in chess are demonstrated in Chapter Two. Secondly, it enables White to strike the first blow in the vital struggle to command the centre of the board. Why this is such a vital issue will begin to become apparent when we examine the powers of the pieces in Chapter One, and even more so when we look at the first elements of strategy, or positional play, in Chapter Three.

In Chapter Four, the three stages of the game are considered: the opening, the middlegame, and the endgame. The variety of ideas governing a game of chess is most clearly to be observed in a consideration of the different sorts of things a player has to think about during each of these stages.

Finally, in Chapter Five, we shall look at

A 8	B 8	C 8	D 8	E 8	F 8	G 8	H 8
A 7	B 7	C 7	D 7	E 7	F 7	G 7	H 7
A 6	B 6	C 6	D 6	E 6	F 6	G 6	H 6
A 5	B 5	C 5	D 5	E 5	F 5	G 5	H 5
A 4	B 4	C 4	D 4	E 4	F 4	G 4	H 4
A 3	B 3	C 3	D 3	E 3	F 3	G 3	H 3
A 2	B 2	C 2	D 2	E 2	F 2	G 2	H 2
A 1	B 1	C 1	D 1	E 1	F 1	G 1	H 1

Fig. 2

three simple games which will, I hope, serve to convince the reader of the complexity, the mystery, and the beauty of chess.

As a preliminary to learning the notation by which chess games are usually recorded, and also to aid the explanation of the moves, Figure 2 illustrates the way in which the squares of the board are numbered according to the international algebraic chess notation.

In this scheme the numbering starts in the same corner as White's queen's rook (the rook nearest White's queen in the initial position). Compare this diagram with

Figure 1. You will see that, in the initial position, White's king stands on e1, his queen on d1, and Black's king is on e8 and his queen on d8, and so on.

Another way of recording chess games is known as the descriptive system. This system is still used in many chess books and you will find details, and a game recorded by this method, in Chapter Five.

The reader should familiarise himself with the following terms before turning to Chapter One.

The centre. This is the name aptly given to the squares d4, e4, d5, e5. Sometimes it is used more loosely to incorporate the twelve squares immediately adjacent to the centre proper as well.

Files. Files are the vertical rows (as represented in Figure 2) a1–a8, b1–b8, c1–c8, and so on.

Ranks. These are the horizontal rows a1–h1, a2–h2, a3–h3, and so on. A player's first rank or back rank is the rank on which his pieces stand in the initial position: for White, a1–h1, and for Black, a8–h8. A player's 'xth' rank is numbered from his back rank; thus the row a4–h4 is White's 4th and Black's 5th rank.

Diagonals. Diagonals are rows of squares adjacent at the corners, e.g. a1–h8, b1–h7, f1–a6, f1–h3, and so on.

The king's side. The king's side is that half of the board to White's right of the line between the d- and e-files, i.e. the squares within the rectangle e1–e8–h8–h1.

The queen's side. The queen's side is the left-hand half of the board as seen by White, i.e. the rectangle a1–a8–d8–d1.

Chapter One
How to Play

How the Men Move

In the initial position (see Figure 1) each player has six different types of men, and different rules govern their movements. However, certain restrictions are shared by all the men. These are:

a) Capturing. If a player captures one of his opponent's men, then the capturing man is placed on the square from which the opponent's man is removed. This rule holds in all cases except that of a pawn captured 'en passant', which is explained later. A player may only capture enemy men, not his own, of course, and capturing is optional (unless it is the only way to escape 'check').

b) Jumping. The knight is the only piece which is allowed to jump over either friendly or hostile pieces. This is because, unlike the other pieces, it does not move in a straight line along the ranks, files or diagonals.

c) Direction of movement. Any piece may move forwards, backwards or sideways. The pawns, however, only move forwards.

Now we are ready to look at the movement of each man individually.

The Pawns

These humble foot soldiers have no less than five ways of aiding their general on the battlefield of the chessboard. Each is depicted in Figure 3. These five options are: the ordinary advance, the initial advance, the promotion, the capture, and the capture en passant.

The ordinary movement of the pawn is one square straight forward along the file on which it stands. This option is available to the white pawns at a4, b2, c7, d4, and g2 in Figure 3, and to the black pawns at e5 and h4. The white pawn at f5 and the black pawn at f6 block each other.

When a pawn stands on its starting square, a player may move it forward two squares on its first move instead of one. Thus the white pawns at b2 and g2 can be moved to b4 and g4 respectively. This privilege is, however, optional, and a player may advance his pawn only one square on its first move if he so wishes.

The white pawn at c7 will reach c8 with its next move. When it does so it is immediately removed from the board and replaced (on c8) by any white piece other than a king. When a player promotes a pawn by attaining the 8th rank he almost invariably promotes it to a queen, which is the strongest piece. It is this possibility of promotion which makes a one-pawn advantage a frequently decisive factor in games between strong players.

The fourth type of move a pawn may make is a capture. The pawn can only capture one square diagonally forward; thus the white pawn at d4 in Figure 3 can capture the black pawn at e5, and the black pawn at e5 can capture the white pawn at d4. The pawns at f5 (white) and f6 (black) are not able to capture each other, but prevent each other from moving forward.

Capturing en passant (French, *in passing*) is illustrated by the pawns at g2 and h4. If a player advances one of his pawns two

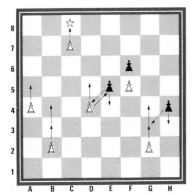

Fig. 3

11

squares on its initial move, and if his opponent has a pawn that could have captured it had it only moved forward one square, then on his next turn, but *only* on his next turn, the second player *may* capture the advanced pawn as if it had indeed only advanced one square.

Thus if White in Figure 3 advances his 'g' pawn two squares to g4, Black may capture it with his 'h' pawn, removing the white pawn from g4 and placing his own on g3.

This complex rule is quite logical. A pawn's initial advance of two squares is a privilege. Ordinarily, however, opposing pawns on adjacent files cannot march past each other without risking capture; thus, if the two-square privilege did not exist, White would have to play his pawn to g3 before moving to g4, and on g3 it would be open to capture by the black pawn at h4.

So the en passant rule is a counter-privilege to prevent a pawn 'sneaking past' with its long first move. Points to remember about the en passant rule:
a) The option of capturing a pawn en passant is available only on the move immediately after the pawn has advanced.
b) The capturing pawn still captures one square diagonally forward, as if the captured pawn had only advanced one square.
c) Pieces cannot capture, nor be captured, en passant.

The Rooks

The rook move is a simple one – rooks travel as far as they like along any unobstructed rank or file (see Figure 4). The rook is a powerful, fast-moving piece, but it requires open lines to exploit its strength. At the beginning of the game, the rooks will be obstructed by friendly men for some time, but later, after some pawns have been exchanged, they will do staunch work.

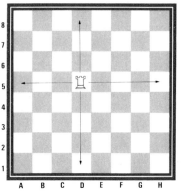

Fig. 4

Notice that on any empty board the rook controls, or can move to, fourteen squares. This is true whether the rook stands at d5 (as in Figure 4) or a1; in this the rook is exceptional, since all the other pieces can control fewer squares from the edge of the board than from the centre.

The Bishops

Bishops move diagonally. Thus the bishop, like the rook, is a long-ranging piece, requiring open lines to conduct its operations. It will be seen from Figure 5 that

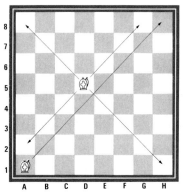

Fig. 5

the bishop controls more squares from a post in the centre than from the sidelines; the bishop at d5 covers thirteen squares, while that at a1 covers only seven.

The bishop can be a handy attacking piece but it has a serious limitation; since it moves diagonally, it is confined to squares of the colour on which it started. Thus any one bishop can only cover half the squares on the board.

In the initial position both players have a 'white-square' and a 'black-square' bishop (see Figure 1). Working together on adjacent diagonals, the two bishops can represent a formidable force, since each complements his partner.

The Knights

A knight makes an L-shaped move, two squares up and one along, in any direction. This is represented schematically by the arrows drawn from the knight at h1 to the squares f2 and g3 in Figure 6. However, the knight move is really a straight-line jump from its starting square to its finishing square, as indicated by the arrows from the knight at d5 to c3, e3, f4, f6, e7, c7, b6, and b4.

It will help you to think of the knight's move in this way because it explains why it can apparently jump over pieces of either colour on the way to its destination. The knight passes between the squares, as it were, and it is therefore the only piece that can be developed before a pawn is moved in the initial position.

It is evident from Figure 6 that the knight controls far more squares from the centre of the board than from the edge (eight from d5, compared with only two from h1). Furthermore, since the knight is a comparatively slow-moving piece, it will

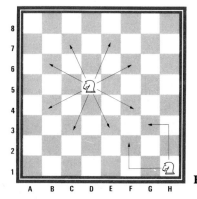

Fig. 6

take longer to go anywhere from the edge of the board than from the centre.

A knight functions more effectively than a bishop or rook in positions without open lines due to its jumping prowess. Also, a knight can reach any square on the board, unlike the colour-bound bishop, though it is slower moving and clumsy beside a rook or bishop on a board with few obstructions.

The Queen

The queen is a very powerful piece, as you will see from Figure 7. She combines the

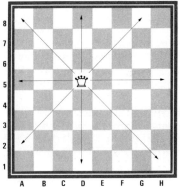

Fig. 7

moves of a rook and a bishop, and moves as far as she likes along any unobstructed line. The queen moves *only* like a rook *or* like a bishop in any one turn though.

From a central square, the queen controls as many as twenty-seven squares on an open board; from the corner, twenty-one squares.

The strength of a queen is sometimes a weakness. Because she is so powerful, she must always flee the attack of an opposing rook, bishop, or knight, as to allow the exchange of a queen for one of these pieces would be a very poor bargain!

The King

The king can move only one square at a time, but in any direction (see Figure 8, centre). Thus it is quite strong at close quarters, but is a slow-moving piece. Like the knight it controls more squares from a central post than from the edge of the board, and can travel more quickly to any square from the former position.

There is a special privilege available to the king known as castling. Once, and only once, during a game, a player may move his previously unmoved king two squares towards a previously unmoved rook, and

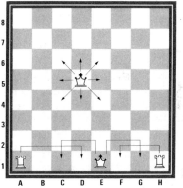

Fig. 8

place the rook on the square which the king has crossed. This is the sole occasion when a player can move two pieces at the same time.

Castling is demonstrated in Figure 8, bottom. The king may be moved from e1 to c1, and the queen's rook from a1 to d1, or the king may be moved from e1 to g1, and the king's rook from h1 to f1. Certain rules govern the privilege of castling:

a) Neither the king nor the rook can have been moved beforehand.

b) The king may not castle at a time when the square he occupies is under enemy

13

attack, *or* if the square he castles onto is under attack, *or* if the square he crosses is under attack.

c) Neither friendly nor enemy pieces may stand between the king and the rook towards which he is castling.

Rules

Now that we have seen how the pieces move, only a few more rules remain to be explained.

Check

When a player's king is attacked by an enemy piece, he is said to be in 'check'. A player who is in check must on his next turn escape, and he has three ways of doing so:
a) If he is able to, he may capture the opposing piece.
b) He may move his king.
c) He may interpose one of his own men between his king and the attacking piece. (Naturally, if the checking piece is a knight, this option will not be available.)

Checkmate!

When a player is unable to escape from check on his next turn, it is 'checkmate', and this is the object of the game. Some

Fig. 9

examples are illustrated in Figure 9.

The board is divided into four quarters, and in each quarter the black king is checkmated. None of the three alternatives outlined previously will enable him to escape check.

Legal moves

If a player is in check but overlooks this, and fails to move out of check, then he does not lose; he must retract the move which he tried to make and instead attend to his king. A legal move is simply one which conforms with the rules.

Touch-and-move

In a serious game of chess it is obligatory for a player to move a piece after he has touched it, if it is legal for him to do so. Also, if he touches an enemy piece which he is able to capture, he must then do so. This rule may of course be waived in a friendly game, but it is a good habit to adhere to it at all times.

If a player wishes to adjust a piece on a square without moving it, he may do so after announcing *J'adoube* (this is French for 'I adjust').

Resignation

If a player sees that ultimate defeat is inevitable and does not wish to play on, he may resign. This usually occurs under two circumstances – either the opponent is about to force checkmate, or the opponent has a large enough material advantage that he must win eventually.

However, you should not bother about resignation while you are playing your first games. You will learn much more by playing on until someone is mated.

Draws

A draw is quite a common occurrence when two experienced players meet, and there are several ways in which a drawn game can arise.
a) Insufficient mating material. King against king, or king and knight against king, or king and bishop against king, are all drawn since no mating position is possible. You should confirm this for yourself. Of course, it is never legal to check with the king, since to do so would involve putting one's own king in check.
b) The fifty move rule. If fifty consecutive moves take place without a pawn being moved or a man being captured on either side, the game is declared a draw. This rule prevents either player from making aimless manoeuvres for ever.
c) Threefold repetition. In the event of the same position recurring three times during a game, with the same player to move, then a draw may be claimed by either side.

A threefold repetition of position is most commonly brought about by a 'perpetual check'. See the position top right in Figure 10.

Although White has a large disadvantage in material, his opponent cannot escape the checks from the white queen. White checks at e8, and Black must move his king to h7. White checks again at h5, and the king must return to g8. White then checks at e8 again,

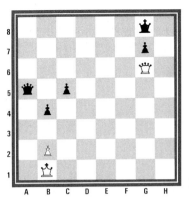

Fig. 10

and his opponent cannot avoid the draw.
d) Stalemate. When a player is unable to make a legal move with any of his remaining pieces (and is not in check although a king move would entail moving into check), then a position of stalemate arises and the game is drawn.

In Figure 11 we see four examples of stalemate. In each case Black has no legal move.
e) Agreed draws. If neither player is satisfied that he or she can win a game, then the players may agree a draw. Sometimes two strong players in a lazy mood will agree a

Fig. 11

draw in a position where chances of victory still remain; while you are learning to play, you should not agree draws too readily.

The Strengths of the Pieces
Situations will often arise during your games when you are in a position to exchange pieces. Whether or not to do so will depend on a variety of factors, but a simple yardstick for the relative values of the pieces is as follows:
pawn = 1 point
knight = 3½ points
bishop = 3½ points

rook = 5 points
queen = 9 points

The bishops and the knights are of about equal strength, and are called the minor pieces. The rooks and the queen are called the major pieces. When a player wins a rook for a bishop or knight, he is said to have 'won the exchange'.

Situations with unbalanced material, e.g. three pawns for a piece, or the exchange for a pawn, or queen and pawn for two rooks, or three pieces for a queen, often produce an interesting struggle.

The Notation
By now, you should be fairly familiar with the algebraic names for the squares. If not, turn back to Figure 2 in the introduction and check on them, since from now on the diagrams will not have letters and numbers next to them.

When a chess game is recorded, the pieces are indicated by capital letters – K for king, Q for queen, R for rook, B for bishop, and N for Knight (Kt is sometimes used, but this might be confused with the symbol for a king). Pawns are not indicated for the sake of economy.

Moves are described by indicating the piece referred to and then the square to which it is moved; the symbol 'x' indicates that an enemy piece is captured on the square to which the piece moves, and the symbol 'ch.' indicates a check.

If you have a chess set, set it up in the initial position of Figure 1 and try to play through the following, very brief game.
1. g4
White moves his 'g' pawn forward two squares.
1. ... e6
Black replies by advancing the pawn in front of his king one square.
2. f3
White advances his 'f' pawn one square.
2. ... Qh4 mate.
Black moves his queen all the way along the diagonal, calling check. White cannot escape check with his next move (you should confirm this for yourself). This final position is shown in Figure 12.

This is the shortest possible game of chess and is known as 'fool's mate'.

Another quick method of winning against an unwary opponent is called 'scholar's mate'. Return your pieces to the starting position again, and play through this game.
1. e4 e5
2. Bc4 Nc6

Fig. 12

Fig. 13

3. Qh5 Nf6
4. Q x f7 mate. See Figure 13.

Sometimes an annotator adds a ! or ? next to a player's move. The ! indicates a good move, the ? a mistake. In our fool's mate example, White's second move deserves a ?, since it allows checkmate; thus 2. f3? In our second example, scholar's mate, Black should have played a different third move, e.g. 3. . . . Qe7 or 3. . . . Qf6. Instead he played 3. . . . Nf6? allowing the mate.

A special symbol is used for castling. 0–0 means 'castles king's side', and 0–0–0 means 'castles queen's side'.

When two pieces of the same type can both move to the same square, and one of them does so, ambiguity is avoided in the notation by specifying the file or rank which the moved piece originally stood on, e.g., if White's back rank is clear except for his rooks, and he plays Re1, the rook moved is specified by Rae1 or Rhe1, whichever it happens to be.

Now that you know how the pieces move, and how to win, lose or draw, you should find someone to play a few friendly games with. This experience will make the rest of this book much more useful to you; the following pages, hopefully, will provide the beginnings of an answer to your question, 'Where did I go wrong!?'

16

Chapter Two
Tactics

Tactics are the move-by-move incidents on the chessboard that demand exact calculation. The most elementary tactical manoeuvre is to attack an enemy piece. If a player leaves a piece where it can be taken for nothing it is said to be *en prise* (French, in a position to be taken). Unless a sacrifice is intended for a concrete reason, it is a gross error to leave a piece *en prise*.

Combinations
Combinations, which are complex tactical manoeuvres, may well involve sacrifices, and require the exact calculation of a series of forcing moves. Such moves are: capture, forcing recapture to avoid material loss, one move threats, or, most forcing of all, a check.

Forks
From the position in Figure 14 White plays his bishop from e4 to d5 with check. Black must then move his king, allowing White to capture the loose rook on b3, i.e., 1. Bd5 ch. K moves 2. B x b3.

This kind of double attack is known as a fork. Figure 15 illustrates an example of a fork with a knight.
White plays: 1. Nf6 ch. K moves 2. N x

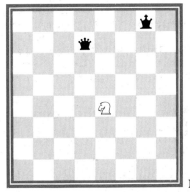

Fig. 15

d7, winning the queen. Many combinations are based on the possibility of such a fork.

Skewers
Another way in which a check can lead to the winning of a piece is shown in Figure 16.

White plays 1. Ra8 ch. and the king must move, allowing 2. R x h8. This device, the prerogative of a rook, bishop, or queen, is known as a skewer, and describes an attack on the king which, when moved to avoid check, leaves the attacker in the position to take another piece.

Fig. 14

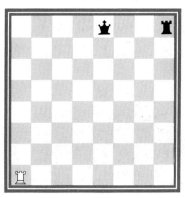

Fig. 16   17

Discovered Checks

Another element of tactical play involving check is the 'discovered check'. A discovered check occurs when a player moves a friendly piece to unmask an attack on the opposing king from a long-range piece (Q, R or B) on the same line.

In Figure 17 White's queen is in line with the black king, masked only by the knight at e5. So 1. Nc6 dis.ch. (a discovered check is usually indicated in this way).

Now if:
a) 1. ... K moves 2. N x d8
b) 1. ... Qe7 2. Q x e7 mate.

Fig. 17

Double Checks

An even more deadly variant of the discovered check is the double check (symbolised as dble. ch.). When a player gives double check, the move of the masking piece gives check as well as revealing a check from the unmasked piece. Faced with such a situation the attacked king is forced to move, if he can, for both checking pieces cannot be captured at once, and defending pieces cannot be interposed along two lines simultaneously.

In Figure 18 White plays 1. Bf6 mate! Although both his pieces are under attack, to

Fig. 18

capture either would still leave Black in check; and no king move is available to Black, since g8 is occupied by his own knight.

Pins

The sensitivity of the king can often be exploited by means other than a direct check. A very common device is the pin. Like the skewer, a pin involves a friendly piece attacking along a line occupied by the enemy king and another piece, but this time the other way round.

In Figure 19 White plays 1. Bd5, and

Fig. 19

Black must lose his queen. The queen cannot escape off the d5–g8 diagonal as Black's king would then be exposed to check.

Decoy Combinations

In Figure 20, White plays 1. Rd8! A pin. But the rook is apparently unprotected; Black has nothing better than 1. ... Q x d8 when White replies 2. Nf7 ch., forking the black king and queen.

This type of combination is known as a decoy combination: the queen is decoyed to a square where she will be lost.

Fig. 20

Another example is given in Figure 21. *Question 1.* How can White win his opponent's queen? (the answers to this and subsequent questions are given at the end of the chapter).

Exploiting Overloaded Pieces

Decoy combinations can be of many types. If a piece is fulfilling two defensive functions at the same time, as is Black's queen in Figure 22, then a combination is in the air.

Without Black's queen on e8, White could either capture the rook on e7 with his queen

Fig. 21

Fig. 22

or play 1. Ra8 ch. Re8 2. R x e8 mate. So the black queen is doing two jobs at once, and that fact can be exploited:
1. Q x e7! Q x e7
2. Ra8 ch. and mate next move.

In this kind of situation, when a piece has more tasks than it can handle, the piece is said to be overloaded.

Undermining Combinations

Sometimes a piece has only one defensive task, as in Figure 23, but can be removed by a sacrifice, leaving another threat indefensible.

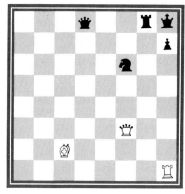

Fig. 23

If Black's knight were not standing at f6, White could continue with 1. R x h7 mate. So White removes the defender:
1. Q x f6 ch! Q x f6
2. R x h7 mate.

This is known as an undermining combination. Incidentally, while it is not so important to remember the vocabulary of tactical terms as it is to visualise the chess moves themselves, it will help you to be aware of the tactical possibilities available if you have names for them.

An undermining combination is not strictly a decoy type, since the initial sacrifice does not involve the lure of an enemy piece onto a less favourable square, but merely replacement of a defender by a piece less suited to the task, as in Figure 23.

The Smothered Mate Decoy

Figure 24 illustrates this decoy.
White exploits his attacking prospects with:
1. Nf7 ch. Kg8
2. Nh6 dble. ch. Kh8
Question 2. Why not 2. . . . Kf8?
3. Qg8 ch! R x g8
4. Nf7 mate.
A similar 'smothered mate' position

Fig. 24   19

appeared in Figure 9 (top right). The decoy motif here involves luring the enemy rook to a square where it obstructs the movement of its own monarch.

The whole combination stemming from Figure 24 is called Philidor's Legacy in honour of the great eighteenth-century chess player and musician who devised it.

Tempo-gaining Decoys
Yet another kind of decoy is played simply to gain time. In an attacking position, every tempo (a move seen as a unit of time) may be vital, as in Figure 25.

Fig. 25

In this position, if White dallies, Black will soon win with a series of checks due to the exposed placement of White's king. But White plays:

1. Rh8 ch! K x h8
2. Qh5 ch. Kg8
3. Qh7 mate.

Here the black king was decoyed onto a square where the attack could continue without loss of tempo.

The Line-clearing Decoy
A further sacrificial motif is the line-clearing sacrifice. Often a player's own man will stand in the way of a decisive attack by his long-range queen, rook, or bishop; a sacrifice then becomes possible, as in Figure 26.

White has a decisive attack after 1. e6!, envisaging 2. d5!, uncovering his bishop at b2 onto Black's 'g' pawn. This position is somewhat more complex than the others we have looked at, in which many pieces were left out. You should play over these variations on your chess set:

a)
1. e6! Q x e6
2. d5! Q x d5
3. R x g7 mate.

b)
1. e6! Be8
2. d5! Qc7
3. d6!
Question 3. Why is this better than 3. R x g7 ch?

Comparatively best for Black is:
c)
1. e6 B x e6
2. d5 Rf1 ch.
Question 4. How would you classify this counter-sacrifice?
3. R x f1 B x d5
4. Qb1 B x h1

Fig. 26

5. R x h1, when White is a piece for a pawn to the good and retains a decisive attack.

Even more complex calculations are frequently required in order to carry out a sacrificial attack against the king successfully. We shall look at some of these later in the chapter.

Combinations to Win Enemy Pieces
The tactical devices we have studied so far have all involved operations against the enemy king, which is perhaps the most exciting aspect of chess. But situations often arise where pins, forks, and skewers can be employed against enemy pieces. These usually involve threatening a minor piece to capture a major one, winning the exchange or more. Four examples appear in Figure 27.

The reader may also like to visualise positions where a knight forks queen and rook, a pawn forks two enemy pieces, or a bishop skewers queen and rook, and so on. However, the employment of a weapon such as the pin of a knight against the queen is not always as effective as a pin against the king, since the pinned piece may still move regardless of loss if bigger things are in the offing. Set up your pieces in the initial position and play through these moves:

20

Fig. 27

1. e4 e5
2. Nf3 d6
3. Bc4 h6
4. Nc3 Bg4

You will now have reached the position shown in Figure 28. In this position White can play:

5. N x e5! B x d1
6. B x f7 ch. Ke7
7. Nd5 mate.

This pretty mate, where White ignores an apparent pin, is known as Legal's Mate after the Frenchman who first unearthed it.

Thus the pin of a piece against the king is

Fig. 28

termed absolute, and against the queen, relative, since the former cannot legally be broken whereas the latter can.

Combinations Used for Promotion

So far we have examined combinations which either led to mate or won material. A third type of combination may occur when one player is threatening to queen (or promote) a pawn; this is in effect a special way of winning material.

In Figure 29 White plays 1. Re5 ch!, forking Black's king and rook, and after 1. ... R x e5 2. b8 = Q, he has the winning

Fig. 29

material advantage of queen against rook (see the section on the endgame in Chapter Four).

A more difficult example of the promotion theme appears in Figure 30.

On 1. c7? Black can stop the pawn with 1. ... Kb7, 1. ... Rc4, or 1. ... Rg8. So, instead, White plays 1. Rd8 ch! with the variations:

a) 1. ... Ka7 2. c7 Rc4 3. c8 = Q R x c8 4. R x c8 and White has a winning material advantage.

b) 1. ... N x d8 2. c7 and the pawn must queen, e.g. 2. ... Kb7 3. c x d8 = Q or 2.

Fig. 30

... Rd4 3. c8 = Q ch. Ka7 4. Qc5 ch., finishing with a fork.

Situations like this, where a pawn attacks a knight with the threat of queening on two squares, occur quite frequently. Notice the element of decoy at work again in Figure 30.

Drawing Combinations

Not all combinations are carried out with the object of winning; sometimes, a player who is on the defensive is able to conjure up a perpetual check or a stalemate (described earlier), and thus salvage a draw from an otherwise poor position.

From Figure 31 White, a long way behind in material, plays 1. R x h6 ch!

Now if Black replies 1.... Kg8, 2. Rh8 is mate.

So 1. R x h6 ch! g x h6 2. Q x h6 ch. Kg8 3. Qg5 ch. Kh7 4. Qh5 ch. Kg7 5. Qg5 ch. and Black cannot escape the barrage of checks. The queen is an especially effective piece for delivering perpetual check, due to the great number of squares she controls.

This combination also demonstrates a theme quite often seen as the prelude to a mating attack: sacrifice of a piece to strip

Fig. 33

Fig. 31

away the protective barrier of pawns round the enemy king.

Our second type of drawing combination is the sacrifice leading to stalemate.

In Figure 32 Black, to play, is a queen for a rook to the bad. However, he plays 1. ... Rf5 ch! and after White's forced reply 2. Q x f5 Black has no move. The squares g7 and g8 are rendered inaccessible by the proximity of White's king, and h7 is controlled by the white queen at f5. Draw!

Figure 33 shows another stalemate combination.

White plays 1. R x c5! attacking the black

queen at c1. If the queen moves away, the threatened discovered check from White's bishop at f2 enables White to win her, e.g. 1. ... Qh6 2. Rh5 dis. ch., etc.

So Black must play 1.... Q x c5, hoping for 2. B x c5 ch. K x c5 when Black wins; he can force the promotion of a pawn from this position.

But instead, after 1. R x c5 Q x c5, White continues 2. Kh1! and Black cannot win. The queen is pinned (if the black king moves she is lost for nothing) and after 2. ... Q x f2 it is stalemate. White's 'a' pawn is blocked and his king has no legal move.

Zugzwang

In the previous, very elegant example we saw a combination of the discovered check, the pin, the stalemate, and an idea called *zugzwang*. This German word means, in chess, the obligation to move at a time when you don't want to.

In the last example Black was in *zugzwang* after 2. Kh1! because he had no good, i.e., winning, move, whereas had it been White's turn to move, White would have lost (you should confirm this for yourself). It is not always an advantage to move next!

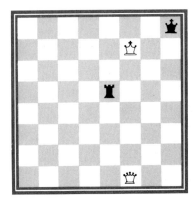

Fig. 32

Fig. 34

White's move in Figure 34 is 1. Bb3! and Black is in *zugzwang*. If 1. . . . g4 2. h x g4, any piece move by Black loses the pinned rook at e6, e.g. 1. . . . Qe8 2. Q x e8 ch. K x e8 3. N x e6, etc.

This pretty position is taken from a game played between two grandmasters in a world championship qualifying tournament. We will see more of *zugzwang* in the endgame section of Chapter Four.

Zwischenzug

Another German word which you are likely to run across is *zwischenzug*. This means, in chess, an 'in-between' move. It sometimes happens that a player makes an apparently forcing move, such as a capture, and his opponent does not recapture at once but interpolates a check or an attack on his queen, completely changing the situation, as in Figure 35.

Black is a rook and two pawns up, but White threatens mate on his next move, i.e., if 1. . . . c1 = Q, there comes 2. Qg7 mate. However, Black has the *zwischenzug* 1. . . . Qe3 ch! forcing 2. N x e3 (2. Q x e3 d x e3 and the black pawn queens) and Black now queens with check, winning, i.e., 2. . . . c1 = Q ch. and now:

Fig. 35

a) 3. Nf1? Q x h6
b) 3. Kg2 Qd2 ch. 4. Kh1 Qe1 ch. 5. Kg2 Qe2 ch. 6. Kh1 (6. Kh3 Q x e3 ch. etc.) 6. . . . Qf3 ch. and White must choose between 7. Kg1 Q x e3 ch. exchanging queens, or 7. Ng2 Qf1 mate.

A *zwischenzug* is, in effect, a tempo-gaining tactical move. Sometimes, when both sides have a piece under attack, a whole series of *zwischenzugs* may take place, as in Figure 36.

This position appears after White's ninth move in a well-known opening line. Black has two ways of trying to exchange a number

Fig. 36

of pieces, desirable because his position may otherwise become cramped. Both methods involve a discovered attack on the knight at d4:

a) 9. . . . Ng4! 10. B x g4! (10. N x c6 is not met by 10. . . . b x c6 11. B x g4 winning a piece, but instead Black plays the *zwischenzug* 10. . . . N x e3. Now a whole series of *zwischenzugs* can follow: 11. N x d8 N x d1 12. N x f7? N x c3! and Black wins) 10. . . . B x d4! (not 10. . . . B x g4? 11. N x c6 and on 11. . . . B x d1 12. N x d8 White wins a piece, or 11. . . . Qd7 12. N x e7 ch!–*zwischenzug*–12. . . . Q x e7 13. Q x g4 winning a pawn) 11. B x d4 B x g4 12. Q x g4 N x d4 with an equal position.

b) 9. . . . Bg4 10. N x c6! and now a series of *zwischenzugs* follow: 10. . . . B x e2 11. N x d8 B x d1 when White does best to play 12. R x d1, since after 12. N x f7? Black has 12. . . . Ng4!, and after 12. N x b7? Black has 12. . . . Bg4, followed by Rab8 leaving White in difficulties.

In these two variations we saw whole series of moves based on the idea, 'we've both got pieces attacked, so if I take something with my attacked piece, and he then captures my piece, and I capture his piece, I've won something!'

A piece which keeps sacrificing itself in this fashion is called a desperado; being doomed, it eats as much as it can. As you will have gathered from the example, desperado combinations are quite intricate and require very precise calculation.

Example Positions

So far in this chapter we have discussed the various elements of tactical play, and examined a few actual combinations. There now follows a selection of more complex examples, and you should try to answer the questions that accompany them.

The artificially constructed position in Figure 37 allows White a truly magnificent sacrificial tour de force.

1. N x g6 ch!

A forcing line clearance.

1. ... f x g6
2. Bf6 ch!

A further forcing line clearance, also involving a self-block decoy of the black queen onto an unfavourable square.

2. ... Q x f6
3. Kd5 dis. ch. Kg5

or 3. ... Bf4 4. R x f4 ch. Q x f4 5. e x f4 with an easily won ending for White.

Fig. 39

Fig. 37

4. h4 ch. Kf5
5. g4 ch! h x g4

Question 5. From the position in Figure 38, White forces checkmate in just two more moves. How?

A much simpler position is shown in Figure 39.

As in the other diagrams, White is playing up the board, and if it were his turn to move he would win by 1. c8 = Q. However Black, to play, has:

1. ... Rd6 ch!
2. Kb5!

If 2. Kb7 Black pins the white pawn with 2.

... Rd7, e.g. 3. Kb8 R x c7 with a draw. And if 2. Kc5 comes 2. ... Rd1!, and on 3. c8 = Q Rc1 ch!, Black wins, or 3. Kb6 Rc1 with a draw; if White plays 2. Ka5 simply 2. ... Rc6 wins the pawn. So the text is the only try.

2. ... Rd5 ch!
3. Kb4!

(3. Kb6 Rd6 ch. repeats the position, and on 3. Kc4 Rd1! etc.)

3. ... Rd4 ch!
4. Kb3! Rd3 ch!
5. Kc2!

Now Black cannot play the R-d1-c1 manoeuvre we saw before, and so all seems lost. However:

5. ... Rd4! See Figure 40.

A cunning reply, so that if White plays 6. c8 = Q we reach the position of Figure 32, when Black can draw by 6. ... Rc4 ch! 7. Q x c4 stalemate!

On 6. Kb3 Black plays 6. ... Rd3 ch., and on 6. Kc3 Rd1, and so the draw seems inevitable – or is it?

Question 6. From the position in Figure 40 White can win quickly. How? (Hint: remember that promotion is not necessarily to a queen.)

And now some examples of the killer

　　　　　Fig. 38

Fig. 40

touch at work in the middlegame.

Figure 41 shows White well on top and his pieces fiercely clustered around Black's king.

Question 7. What is the most forcing continuation in Figure 41, winning at least a rook?

Again, White can win by pedestrian means in Figure 42, e.g., 1. Q x b5. But there is something better.

Question 8. The combination White plays in Figure 42 can be described as a double decoy followed by a fork. What series of four forcing checks wins a piece?

Fig. 43

Fig. 41

Fig. 44

Fig. 42

In Figure 43 White is two pawns behind but his pieces are aggressively posted. However, if 1. N x f7 Black replies 1. ... Be6 with adequate defence.

Question 9. How does White bring his pressure against f7 to fruition in Figure 43?

In our next example in Figure 44 Black has his opponent in a crossfire of pins.

From this position Black continued 1. ... c x d4!

Question 10. How did Black exploit pinning and forking possibilities to win a pawn after 2. N x d4?

The position of Figure 45 arose after

White had sacrificed a rook and a bishop to strip away the pawn cover from the enemy king. There followed:

1. Bf4?

Threatening both Be5 ch. and Rh1 mate. However, Black now produced a double sacrifice to save himself, starting with a line-blocking move:

1. ... Bh3 ch!
2. K x h3 R x f4!
3. g x f4 Qg8

Forcing the exchange of queens, Black produces a difficult but winning endgame.

Question 11. What should White have played

Fig. 45 25

on move 1, and remember to look for tricky Black defences?

Answers

1. White plays 1. Bd5 ch! forking king and queen, and forcing the reply 1. . . . Q x d5 when 2. Nf6 ch. is a second and winning fork.

2. If 2. . . . Kf8 comes 3. Qf7 mate.

3. On 3. R x g7 ch., Black replies 3. . . . Q x g7 4. B x g7 K x g7 with rook and bishop for the queen. After 3. d6!, however, he must allow White to win his queen for a pawn, since to move his queen off the second rank (where it has no safe square) would permit 4. R x g7 mate.

4. 2. . . . Rf1 ch. is a tempo-gaining sacrifice, forcibly decoying the white rook off the g-file since 2. . . . B x d5 fails to 3. R x g7 mate.

5. White continues 6. Rf4 ch!–the third self-block decoy–6. . . . B x f4 7. e4 mate! A glorious combination.

6. White plays 6. c8 = R! Ordinarily, K + R *v* K + R is, of course, a draw, but here Black's pieces are very badly placed. White threatens mate by 7. Ra8 ch. etc, and 6. . . . Rc4 ch. 7. R x c4 leaves Black's king with a move–7. . . . Ka2. So after 6. c8 = R! Black has only 6. . . . Ra4 when 7. Kb3! is a killer–both Black's rook and mate by 8. Rc1

are threatened. An unusual kind of fork!

7. White wins by 1. Rf8 ch! and if 1. . . . R x f8, 2. B x g5 ch. forces mate. On 1. . . . Be8 2. Q x c7 ch. K x c7 3. R x h8, etc. And on 1. . . . Ke7, 2. N x c8 ch! wins Black's queen.
If 1. Q x c7 ch. (not followed by 1. . . . R x c7? 2. R x h6! R x h6 3. Nf7 ch., etc.) 1. . . . K x c7, 'only' the exchange is lost.

8. The continuation is 1. Ne5 ch. Kg7 2. R x e7 ch! Q x e7 3. Q x h8 ch! K x h8 4. N x g6 ch., followed by 5. N x e7, leaving White a piece up.

9. White plays 1. R x d8! R x d8 2. Q x f7 ch. Kh8 3. Qg8 ch. R x g8 4. Nf7 mate. This combination relies on undermining and the Philidor's Legacy theme.

10. Black played 2. . . . N x e3 3. f x e3 (forced) 3. . . . R x e3! Now if 4. R x e3 B x d4 5. Rae1 Rae8 6. Kf2 R x e3, etc. Black wins the K + P ending, having an extra pawn. So White tried 4. Rd1 and eventually lost because of his pawn minus.

11. White should continue 1. Be3!, whereupon 1. . . . Bh3 ch! 2. K x h3 d4! is met, not by 3. Kg2 Qd5 ch!, but 3. Rh1! and if 3. . . . Qd5 4. B x d4 ch! Q x d4 5. Kg2 mate. If you saw all this you did very well indeed! Incidentally, the defence 1. . . . B x g5 fails to 2. Rh1 ch. Bh4 3. Bd4 ch. Q or R f6 4. R x h4 mate.

Chapter Three
Strategy

In the last chapter we discussed only positions that required exact calculation of a series of moves. But, for a large part of the time, the situation on the chessboard is not suited to move-by-move analysis. The purely tactical player will frequently find himself bewildered with nothing to calculate and with no understanding of strategic possibilities.

Our discussion of strategy will be split into two parts: general principles and planning.

General Principles
General principles are of two sorts: there are principles covering piece play and those covering pawn play.

A warning should be sounded at this point. General principles are not enough on their own; you might follow them throughout a game and still lose. When it is your turn to move, use them to decide what moves might be good, and then calculate the precise consequences of each until you find the best one.

Principles of Piece Play
One vital maxim should always be borne in mind: 'Seek active play for all your pieces throughout the game!'

Most of the following principles of piece play are developments of this maxim.

Occupy Open Lines
Your long-ranging pieces (rooks, bishops and queen) require open files and diagonals in order to exert their full effect on the enemy position. In the opening, one rook will usually be developed by castling. When one or more pawns have been exchanged, the rooks must hurry to occupy the open files.

Throughout the game such rooks are a perpetual harassment to the opposition, as in Figure 46.

Here White's mastery of the open file and the availability of entry squares (b5, b6, b7) into the opposing position weigh far more heavily than his lost queen pawn.

Play continued 1. . . . Bc5 2. Qb5 ch! Ke7 3. c x d4 N x d4 4. Qb7 ch!

Now on 4. . . . Q x b7 5. R x b7 ch. and 6. B x d4, White wins a piece. So Black is forced to obstruct his king's rook, i.e. 4. . . . Kf8 5. Ng5!

White cannot win a piece by 5. Q x a7 because of the *zwischenzug* 5. . . . N x f3 ch! 6. Kg2 B x a7 with defensive chances.

Fig. 46

Instead he sets up a powerful threat against Black's 'f' pawn with 5. . . . Q x b7 6. R x b7.

The object of the player whose rooks occupy open files is to penetrate deep into the enemy position when the pieces defending the entry squares have been exchanged or forced away. White pursued this possibility until he reached Figure 47.

Now White threatens R x e6! due to the pin exerted by the other rook. Black actually tried 1. . . . g5? and should have lost after 2. R x e6.

On 1. . . . Re8 there can follow: 2.

27

Fig. 47

Fig. 49

Bc5 a4 3. Rd6 Rc8 4. Bb4 Rc2 ch. 5. Kf3! R x h2 6. R6d7 and Black can no longer defend.

Bishops also require open lines, and you will often find these pieces referred to as 'good' or 'bad'. A good bishop is one that is not obstructed by pawns and can sight targets in the enemy camp. A bad bishop, on the other hand, is one that is obstructed by a barrier of pawns, usually friendly. Figure 48 is an example of a very bad bishop.

Black's bishop on g7 is a miserable piece. White's plan consists of preparing the breakthrough b4 and c5, creating open lines

Fig. 48

on the Q-side where his space advantage and virtual extra piece should tell in his favour. Play went:
1. Bd1! Na6 2. Ba4 Qd8

Now White's white-square bishop is outside the barrier of friendly pawns and pressing down into the black position.
3. Nge2 h6 4. Ng3! eyeing the f5 square. 4. ... Bh8?

Black would have done better to manoeuvre ... Rf7 and ... Bf8, hoping to revive the bishop when White breaks open the Q-side. From now on White's plan developed logically until Figure 49 was

reached.

White has prepared a breakthrough combination to exploit the incarceration of his opponent's bishop.
1. d6! c x d6 2. Nd5 Ne6
Or 2. ... Qd8 3. c7 Qf8 (else 4. N x f6 mate!) 4. N x b6 and wins. If 2. ... Rb8, White plays 3. Ra1 and wins by penetrating to a6 or a7 with his rook.
3. Nf5 Ra3 4. N x b6 R x f3 5. Q x d6 Q x d6 6. N x d6 Ra3 7. Nd5
And Black was helpless against White's advanced pawns. (Note: the breakthrough combination played here led not to material but positional profits.)

The next example in Figure 50 shows bishops, rooks and queen in coordination along several lines where White has weakened his position through incautious advances. Play went:
1. ... Bf5! 2. B x f4 Be4
A marvellous bishop, perpetually dangerous to White's king.
3. h4 Qd7! 4. Kh2 Rac8

Now White cannot challenge the file, since 5. Racl R x cl 6. R x cl Qg4! wins Black a piece. So White prevents the threat of ... Rc2.
5. Ne1 Rc4! 6. Rd1 Rfc8 7. Rg3 Bd4

Fig. 50

Black's threats cannot be met. White gave up a pawn with 8. Bd2 R x d4 9. B x b4 R x b4, but to no avail; the black pieces were still the more active.

Further points to remember about your long-range pieces:
a) If you have two bishops *v* bishop and knight or two knights, open up the position (i.e., exchange pawns) to develop the full power of the bishops.
b) Usually, a queen cannot maintain control of open lines early in the game since she will be attacked along those lines by lesser enemy pieces. However, the number

Ne6 7. B x e6 d x e6 8. Ne8!
And Black resigned, having no answer to the threats of Q x f8 ch. and B x g7 ch. Notice how White's manoeuvres involved the central squares (3. Ne4, 6. Bd4).

Another example is shown in Figure 52.

Instead of the natural and centralising 1. Rad1, White decentralised his knight by 1. Ne1? f x e5! 2. B x e5.

It would have been better for White to be able to recapture with the knight. Now, with his next two moves, White cedes all control of the central white squares (e4 and d5) to his opponent.

Fig. 51   **Fig. 52**

of lines available to the queen increases as pieces are exchanged (the same also applies, to a lesser extent, with rooks).
c) Opposite-coloured bishops occur when each side has only one bishop left and the bishops control different colour squares. Such bishops are a valuable attacking factor in the middlegame, since the attackers outnumber the defenders on squares of one colour. In the endgame, however, opposite-coloured bishops are regarded as a considerable drawing factor, since it is difficult to force pawns across the squares controlled by the opposing bishop.

Centralise!
Centralisation of the pieces almost invariably means greater coordination and effectiveness. Figure 51 is an example of one side completely dominating the centre.

In this position, White totally controls the whole centre. Black's pieces are effectively split in two, and White wins rapidly by switching all his pieces to the king's side, which his opponent cannot emulate because he is so cramped.
1. Ng5! Rf8 2. Qh4 h6 3. Ne4 B x e5
Black bids for freedom.
4. Q x e7 Bg7 5. Nf6 ch. Kh8 6. Bd4!

2.... Nf6 3. B x c6? Q x c6 4. c3 Ne4! 5. Bd4 Rf5!
Preparing to double rooks on the f-file. Now White should regain some control on the white squares with 6. f3, driving away Black's knight. Instead, he tries to recentralise his own knight, only to succumb to a combination made possible by Black's agile, centrally-posted knight.
6. Nd3 Ng5!
Threat 7.... Nh3 mate, and if 7. h4 Nf3 ch., 8. Kg2 or Kh1 N x d4 dis. ch. is devastating. So White must concede a pawn.
7. f3 R x f3! 8. Nf4? R x f4 9. R x f4 Nh3 ch. 10. Kf1 Qh1 ch.
And White resigned, for on 11. Bg1 follows 11.... Q x g1 mate. Notice also the effectiveness of the queen in control of the long diagonal after the exchange of bishops.

You should attend to the centre throughout the game for a variety of reasons:
a) The opening sees a fight for the centre. There are two ways of handling the opening; one is to occupy the centre with pawns supported by pieces. This is known as the classical approach. Figure 53 illustrates the classical centre.

Here White has a strong centre, which his opponent has allowed him to build through   29

Fig. 53

Fig. 55

a series of time-wasting pawn advances on the queen's side.

Another approach to the centre in the opening is not to occupy it at once, but to exert pressure on it from the wings by piece attacks combined with flanking advances of the 'c' and 'f' pawns. This is known as hypermodern strategy. In Figure 53 Black had neglected the centre entirely; in Figure 54, however, Black is ready to encircle his opponent's classical centre.

Black played 1. ... Nfd7!, both revealing his bishop at g7 and preparing the flanking blow ... c5. There followed:

Fig. 54

2. Qc2 c5! 3. Qa2 Qc7 4. Nf1 d5!
Blocking the diagonal of White's bishop and queen. 5. e x d5 is met by the *zwischenzug* 5. ... c4 before recapturing at d5. So:
5. e5 f6!
Undermining the White centre from all directions.
6. f4 f x e5 7. f x e5 Nc4 8. Nf4 Rae8 9. Bd1 c x d4 10. c x d4
Reaching the position of Figure 55. White has allowed his pieces to become very tangled, whereas Black's purposeful manoeuvres in the centre have built the tension to an explosive pitch.

Black broke through with:
10. ... Nd x e5! 11. d x e5 Q x e5
Threatening both N x e3 and Q x a1.
12. Bc5 R x f4 13. R x f4 Q x f4 14. Rb1 Na3!
Discovering an attack on the knight at f1 with the bishop at a6, and so winning the exchange. With the exchange and two pawns extra, Black soon won.

Games in which one side (usually White) adopts a classical set-up and the opponent, a hypermodern formation can give rise to quite fascinating struggles. However, whichever sort of formation you choose to adopt, always remember to attend to the centre.

b) In the middlegame, attacks on the flank can only succeed if the attacker has a strong centre.

In Figure 56, White has just relaxed his grip on the centre by Rdg1?, in order to pursue a king's-side attack. Now Black strikes back in typical fashion – by breaking open the centre.
1. ... c5! 2. d x c5 B x c5! 3. Ng4
Not 3. Q x c5? Rc8 pinning the queen.
Instead White threatens 4. Nh6 ch. g x h6
5. g x h6 dis. ch. Ng6 6. Qg7 mate, but the knight move is a further decentralisation.

Fig. 56

3. ... Ng6 4. Kb1 Bb4 5. Qc2
Or 5. Qd3 Bc6!, forcing the exchange of
queens and the end of White's attack. This
was comparatively best, however.
5. ... Rc8 6. Qe2 Bc6 7. Rd1 Qb6 8.
f3 b x a4 9. Ba2 Qb7! 10. Rh3 a3!
Reaching the position in Figure 57. Now
it is the white king which will succumb
first.
  Play continued:
11. h5 Bb5 12. Qg2 N x f4 13. e x f4
Red8! 14. R3h1 Bd3 ch. 15. R x d3
  As a result of Black's central control,
White must yield the exchange as 15. Ka1

Fig. 58

Fig. 57

Fig. 59

a x b2 ch. and 16. ... Bc3 is devastating.
15. ... R x d3 16. Nf6 ch. Kh8! 17.
Ne4 Bd2!
And White resigned, as mate follows
shortly, e.g., 18. b3 R x b3 ch., etc.
  Notice how Black seized the c- and d-files
with decisive effect, whereas White's
threatening build-up in Figure 56 never
went anywhere. The strength of the
long-range pieces on open lines is also
apparent in this example.
  When you look at the illustrative games in
Chapter Five, you will again observe the
rule 'attack on the flank only if you have a
strong centre!' in action.
c) In the endgame, all pieces – and
especially the king – should be centralised
(rooks may be exempted from this
principle – see the comment on rooks in
Chapter One).
  Figure 58 shows an example in which
White has a beautiful access route to the
centre across the black squares. Play went:
1. Kf2! Rc8 2. Ke3! Rc3 3. Kd4! R x a3
4. Kc5! Ra4 5. Kd6! Bc6
On 5. ... Bc8 6. Kc7 wins the bishop.
6. Rf4 a5 7. K x e6 R x b4 8. R x b4 a x b4
Reaching the position illustrated in Figure
59.

White has sacrificed a pawn to secure a
completely dominating position for his
king.
  The finish was:
9. Ke7 Kg7 10. h4 Kg8 11. e6 Kg7 12.
g3 Kg8 13. Kd8 Kg7 14. h5! g x h5
On 14. ... Kf6 15. e7 Kf7, the manoeuvre
B–e2–f3 x d5 ch. is decisive.
15. e7 Kf7 16. Bf5
And Black has no defence to the threat of
Bd7 followed by e8 = Q; he played 16.
... b3 and resigned after 17. c x b3.
  By now you should be firmly convinced of
the necessity for centralisation of your
pieces. This will ensure you greater
coordination, better attacking chances, and
immunity from attacks by your opponent.
  A few points about the knights should
now be noted: they function especially well
in blocked positions, a knight against a bad
bishop is often a decisive advantage, and
they benefit probably more than any other
piece from being centralised.
  A good example of the strengths of the
knights has already appeared in Figure 49;
you should play through this position again,
looking carefully at the role of the
centralised knights. Figure 60 illustrates
another field day for these pieces.

31

Fig. 60

Play went:
1. Nd6 Qb6 2. Ra2 Kb8 3. Rea1 Rf8 4. Qe4 f6

And White's dominating centre, control of the a-file, and unassailable knights gave him the opportunity for 5. Ra6! B x a6 6. R x a6 Qd8 7. R x c6, with the unstoppable threat of 8. Na6 ch. and 9. Rc8 dble. ch. mate.

Knights also have their drawbacks, however; in open positions, lacking secure central posts, a knight can be driven back and find itself unable to participate at all. See, for example, the continuation of Figure 50.

When to Exchange
You will often be presented with the dilemma of whether or not to exchange pieces. It is not good policy to exchange simply 'because it's there'; you should only do so for a definite reason. For example:
a) Exchange so as not to lose time or space by retreating.
b) Exchange in order to maintain control of a key square, file or diagonal.
c) If your pieces are cramped, exchanges will relieve the pressure.
d) Exchange your opponent's defending pieces if this allows you to make further ground.

In other words, exchanges, like your other moves, should be directed towards a concrete positional or tactical goal.

When to Attack
The first recognised world champion, William Steinitz, who lived in the second half of the nineteenth century, formulated the concept of 'balance of position'. Usually both players will control an equal share of the key lines, the centre, etc., and according to Steinitz, you should not attack until this equilibrium has been disturbed. He also observed:
a) Premature attacks will be repulsed and the 'attacker' will find himself disorganised.
b) When you hold the advantage, you must attack, otherwise your advantage will slip away.
c) The direction of an attack should be dictated by the factors which disturbed the equilibrium in the first place.

Principles of Pawn Play
Philidor, who we have already met in Chapter Two (see Figure 24), once said, 'Pawns are the soul of chess'. This pronouncement, made in the infancy of chess theory, is still as true today.

Since the pawns can only move forwards, their advances must be timed with great care. Too many early pawn advances can leave a maze of weaknesses in their rear (refer again to Figure 50 for an example, and also see illustrative game No. 2 in Chapter Five).

Also, since the pawns cannot capture straight ahead, the square immediately in front of a pawn can become a strongpoint for the enemy men. Thus pawns function most effectively if they are kept abreast. Pawns advancing together in a phalanx can be a powerful attacking weapon, forcing back the enemy pieces and clearing lines for your own.

In Figure 61, Black generates a powerful king-side attack by advancing his pawn phalanx.
1. . . . f5! 2. b x c6 b x c6 3. Bc3 Nf6 4. Ng1?
Trying to defend before he is attacked, but the move is unnecessarily decentralising. Better is to leave the knight on f3 until Black plays . . . e4, when the knight can go to the central post d4.
4. . . . d5! 5. Bb4 Qf7 6. c x d5 c x d5 7. Nb3 f4! 8. Nc5 e4!

Fig. 61

We have now reached the position shown in Figure 62.

This pawn sacrifice, unleashing Black's bishop at b8, leads to the rapid destruction of the white king's position.
9. d x e4 d x e4 10. B x e4 f x g3 ch. 11. f x g3 B x g3 ch. 12. K x g3 Nh5 ch! 13. Kh2 Qc7 ch! 14. Kh1 Ng3 ch. 15. Kg2 Nh4 ch! 16. Kf2 Qf4 ch! 17. Nf3 R x c5! 18. Bd2 N x e4 ch.

White resigned, for 19. Ke1 comes 19. ... Ng2 ch. 20. Kd1 Q x d2 ch. 21. N x d2 R x d2 mate.

The continuation after the pawn phalanx

win is in sight.
7. K x f4 Ra3 8. Ne1 h3 9. Nf3 Kd7 10. Nd4 Nb6?

A mistake, but the pawns were fast becoming indefensible. If Black does nothing, White can simply manoeuvre N–f5–g3 and K–g4 x h3: the move played allowed 11. R x c7 ch. K x c7 12. Nb5 ch. and White won.

It is important to remember, if you or your opponent have an isolated pawn, that control of the square in front of the pawn is worth having. The player with the isolated pawn will seek to advance it; the other player

Fig. 62

disappeared is a typical result of such an attack, but what you should especially notice is the plan started in Figure 61: f5!, followed by d5! followed by f4! followed by e4!, with decisive effect.

Usually the pawn structure in such a position remains fairly constant for long periods. As we have already noted, it is advantageous to keep pawns abreast of each other, or serious static weaknesses may result. The most serious of these weaknesses occurs when there is no possibility of defending the square in front of a pawn, and an enemy piece can then occupy it.

Isolated Pawns
A pawn which has no friendly pawns on adjacent files is said to be isolated. An example is Figure 63, and two vital factors are quickly apparent: the square in front of Black's isolated 'c' pawn is an ideal post for a white piece, and when the pawn is attacked Black's pieces are tied down defending it. Play went:
1. Nb4 Na8 2. g3 Ra4 3. g x f4 e x f4 4. Nd3 f x e3 ch. 5. K x e3 Ke7 6. f4! g x f4 ch.

Now all Black's pawns are isolated; the

will seek to blockade and win it.

Backward Pawns
A pawn whose comrades on adjacent files have both advanced leaving it behind is, like the isolated pawn, defensible only by pieces. If the pawn is backward on an open file, it can become a particular target for attack, as in Figure 64.

Here Black's 'd' pawn is backward and the attack against it forces Black to make further concessions.
1. Rfd1 0–0 2. B x f6 g x f6
(Remember that the 0–0 symbol means

Fig. 64   33

'castles king's side'. See end of Chapter One.)

Already Black has to accept a disastrous weakening of his king's side, since 2. ...
B x f6 allows 3. Q x d6.
3. Nh4! Re8 4. Nf5 Bf8

Now White can win by 5. N x d6, picking up the backward pawn, but in view of the 'reflex weaknesses' Black has created on the king's side in his efforts to save the pawn, White decides to avoid the exchange of pieces and attacks instead.
5. Qg3 ch! Kh8 6. Qh4
Threat R–d3–h3.
6. ... Bd7 7. N x d6 B x d6 8. R x d6
Qe7 9. Nd5!
And Black resigned, since on 9. ... Q x
d6 10. N x f6 he must give up his queen to prevent mate, e.g. 10. ... Kg7 11. Qg5
ch. Kh8 (or 11. ... Kf8 12. N x h7 mate!)
12. Qh6 and the only defence is 12. ... Q x
f6 13. Q x f6 ch., leaving White with a comfortable queen and two pawns against rook and bishop.

Notice how all Black's troubles stem from the backward pawn and White's control of the d5 square. Had Black's 'e' pawn been at e6 instead of e5, White could not have won so easily; control of d5 and, later, of f5 would

In Figure 65 White is superficially more active; in fact he is in very serious difficulties, thanks to the doubled 'c' pawns. White cannot play 1. R x g7? because ...
Re1 mate, and the doubling of his pawns presents the following problems:
a) Black will exchange White's 'a' pawn for his 'b' pawn, creating a 'passed' pawn on the a-file (see section, later in this chapter, on passed pawns). This is a result of White's 'b' pawn having been deflected to the c-file.
b) White will have great difficulty moving his pieces to prevent Black's 'a' pawn from queening, because his manoeuvrability is limited by his own doubled pawns.
c) The pawns themselves are both weak, requiring protection by pieces if they are attacked.

The game went:
1. a5 b6! 2. a x b6 ch. N x b6 3. R x e8
N x e8 4. Be2 a5! 5. Nd1 Ba4! 6. Be1 Bb3
7. Ne3 Nf6

In the position now reached in Figure 66, White is already at full stretch, and the entry of Black's other knight must be decisive.
8. Bd3 Ne4 9. B x e4 f x e4 10. Bd2
B x c4 11. g4
A last try, White has planned a combination to eliminate Black's 'a' pawn:

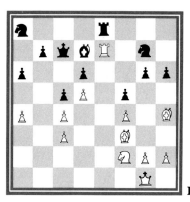

Fig. 65

Fig. 66

not have been possible.

In fact, had Black's pawn been at e6 in Figure 64 there could have happened: 1.
Rfd1 0-0 2. B x f6 B x f6! and on 3.
Q x d6 Q x d6 4. R x d6 B x c3 5. b x c3
B x e4 and Black would be on top.

Doubled Pawns
Two friendly pawns standing on the same file are said to be doubled. Such pawns do not protect, but obstruct, each other. It is quite common for doubled pawns to be isolated or backward as well, in which event they are a serious weakness.

11. ... B x d5 12. c4 B x c4 13. B x a5 Bf7

Black won shortly, in view of his extra pawns. The weakness of the doubled pawns shows very clearly in this example; they proved both a hindrance and a liability. If you refer back to Figure 64 you will see that Black acquired doubled pawns in that example as well; again, the pawns proved a gruesome weakness, and the final combination was based on the fact that these pawns cut off the friendly pieces from defence of the black king.

Let us look now at some more features of pawn play.

Pawn Chains

Pawn chains are rows of diagonally adjacent friendly pawns. Usually, pawn chains are interlocking, i.e. both sides have a pawn chain directly obstructing each other, as in Figure 67.

In such positions, with the centre solidly blocked, each player should seek play on the wing where he has more space. This is usually achieved by attacking the base of the opponent's pawn chain by advancing the next pawn along, e.g., in Figure 67 White's plan is the advance c4–c5, and Black aims at f5.

Fig. 67

Generally it would be antipositional to attack the head of the chain, since a backward pawn may result; e.g., in Figure 67 1. f4 e x f4 would leave White's 'e' pawn and the e5 square very weak.

Figure 68 shows a typical pawn-chain struggle. Black has a completely winning position simply because he can attack the base of White's pawn chain (d4) whenever he wishes. White has mishandled his pawns on the king's side and can obtain no compensating breakthrough to exploit his local space advantage there. Play went:
1. Bd2 Na5 2. Nc1 Kd7! 3. 0–0 Rb8! 4.

Fig. 68

Qf3 Rhc8 5. Qe2 Nf5! 6. Be1 c5!

White has absolutely no defence to the threats along the c-file.
7. Qf2 B x d3 8. c x d3 c x d4 9. c x d4 Rc2!

And White resigned, rather than trying to find a move in a hopeless situation, e.g., 10. Qf3 Q x d4 ch., or 10. Ne2 Nb3, or 10. Bd2 R x d2! 11. Q x d2 Q x d4 ch. and 12. . . . Q x a1.

Weak Squares

We have already seen the weakness of a square in front of an isolated or backward pawn. Such squares provide a perfect base for enemy pieces. Similarly, weak squares may appear even when the pawns are not isolated or backward, as in Figure 69.

Here White has a superb 'blockade' square at d4, from where his knight exerts great pressure, and supports the natural advance b5 attacking the base of Black's pawn chain. If Black exchanges on e5 White will obtain a second dominating blockading piece on that square too. There followed:
1. b5 Rf7 2. Rb1 Bc7 3. Qd3 a x b5 4. a x b5 c x b5 5. Q x b5 Ref8 6. c6 Bc8 7. Ra1 f x e5 8. B x e5 B x e5 9. R x e5
See Figure 70.

Fig. 69

Fig. 70   35

Now White controls both the weak squares in front of Black's pawns, with crippling effect; Black's minor pieces have no scope whatsoever, and White will penetrate decisively via the a-file.
9. ... Qg6 10. Ra8 Rc7 11. Qb6 Qf7 12. Re2! Qf4 13. g3 R x c6?
Loses, but after 13. ... Qd6, 14. Ne5 followed by Nb5 is crushing.
14. Q x c6 Q x f3 15. Q x c8 Qd3 16. Qc5
Black resigned: he is a rook down.

Sometimes one side will have not just one or two weak squares but a whole complex of weak squares. This most frequently occurs with interlocking pawn chains, controlling rows of squares, or when one bishop has been exchanged leaving the squares of the colour it used to control without adequate protection, as in Figure 71.

White has just won two rooks and a bishop for his queen, but suffers from a fatal weakness on the black squares which enables Black to regain a rook at once. After this, White is left with only his 'bad' bishop, and the black king will be able to march along the complex f6–g5–f4–e3 or g3 with impunity.
Play went:

Fig. 71

1. ... Qh4 ch. 2. Kf1 a1 = Q ch! 3. R x a1 Qh1 ch. 4. Kf2 Q x a1 5. Rc2 Kf6! 6. Kg2 Kg5! 7. R x c5 Qb2 8. Kf1
Not 8. Kf2? Qd4 ch. Black owns the black squares!
8. ... Kf4! 9. Bd1 Qd4 10. Rc1 Kg3
And White is defenceless, e.g., 11. Ke1 Qe3 ch.; in fact, the game ended 11. Rc2 Q x d1 mate.

For other examples where one side can attack without obstruction over a whole complex of squares, refer back to Figures 50, 51 and 58, and also to illustrative game No. 3.

Pawns Round the King
It is important to keep a row of pawns in front of the king for protection. Usually both sides will castle at an early stage, since the centre pawns are advanced in the opening, and the pawns in front of the castled king can be arrayed in a variety of ways, as in Figure 72.

All three pawns unmoved, as in the bottom left quadrant, is regarded as the best defensive formation. The formation shown in the bottom right quadrant is usually quite safe as well. With a knight's pawn moved, as in the top right quadrant, a complex of

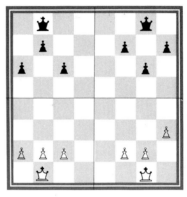

Fig. 72

weaknesses can arise (e.g., here f6, g7, h6)–see the continuation from Figure 52. With a bishop occupying the hole on g7, however, this formation is quite frequently seen as the bishop safeguards the weaknesses at f6 and h6.

The structure shown in the top left quadrant of the figure, with rook's pawn and bishop's pawn both advanced, involves a complex of weaknesses–here a5, b6, a7, and c5.

In the absence of one or more of the defensive pawns, attacking lines may be opened to the hostile forces; and with one of the pawns moved, it may become possible for the opponent to break open lines of attack by advancing a pawn on the adjacent file, as in Figure 73.

With both kings castled on opposite sides, a race will take place to see whose attack strikes home first. White aims at b4, a4, and b5; Black should strive for g5, g4, in order to open lines against the king.
There followed:
1. Rfb1! f5 2. Nc4 Re8 3. b4 f4 4. Bd2 g5! 5. h4!
Breaking the force of Black's counterattack, since on 5. ... g x h4 6. Qh3!, the exchange of queens leaves White far better developed,

Fig. 73

while the extra doubled pawn counts for little. On 5. a4? g4!, Black's attack would have come in first.

5. ... g4 6. Qd1 b5?

To drive White's knight from its strong post, but now White will open lines even faster when he plays a4.

The position now reached is shown in Figure 74.

7. Na5 Nf6 8. g3!

Further consolidating the king's side before commencing the decisive attack.

8. ... Bh6 9. Nb3 Qh7 10. a4! Rd8 11. a x b5 f x g3

Fig. 74

Or 11. ... a x b5 12. Nc5!-threat Ra8 mate-12. ... Kb8 13. Ra8 ch! K x a8 14. Ra1 ch. Kb8 15. Ra8 ch! K x a8 16. Qa1 ch. Kb8 17. Qa6 and 18. Qb7 mate. A double line-clearance sacrificial possibility based on the line-opening manoeuvre b4, a4 and a x b5.

12. f x g3 N x e4

Desperation, which White ignores ...

13. R x a6! B x d2 14. b x c6!

And there is no defence to the threat of Ra8 mate, e.g., 14. ... Kb8 15. Rba1, etc.

So remember–beware weakening pawn advances in front of the castled king!

Passed Pawns

A passed pawn is a pawn which has no enemy pawns standing on the same or adjacent files between itself and its queening square; such pawns must be prevented from queening by pieces only, and are often a decisive factor.

In Figure 75 both sides have two passed pawns, White at c5 and e5, and Black at d5 and a7. White is winning, however–his 'c' pawn is well advanced, and the knight standing at d4 blockades Black's 'd' pawn and controls the c6 square (e.g., 1. ... Nc6? 2. Bb5!). It is Black's turn to move.

Fig. 75

1. ... Qa4 2. Bb5 Qa3 3. c6! Bc8 4. c7! Ne6 5. N x e6 B x e6 6. Bc6!

And White wins: 6. ... Rc8 7. Bb7, etc. We have already encountered passed pawns, e.g. Figures 59, 66, 70. In the endgame passed pawns are a particularly effective weapon (see Chapter Four).

Candidates and Majorities

A candidate is a pawn which is not passed but which will become so by advancing in conjunction with a colleague and exchanging off the opposing pawn; in Figure 76 White's 'c' pawn is a candidate, as

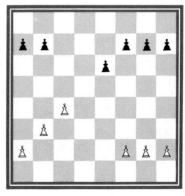

Fig. 76 37

is Black's 'e' pawn. White plays b4, c5, b5, c6 to create a passed pawn, and similarly Black advances his 'e' and 'f' pawns.

A pawn majority in the centre or on either wing is simply a local superiority in pawn numbers; in Figure 76 White has a queen's-side pawn majority and Black, a king's-side majority.

A healthy pawn majority will contain a candidate, as with the majorities in Figure 76. In Figure 77, however, Black's queen's-side majority is crippled.

White can play f4, e5, f5 and e6, etc., but Black has no way of capitalising on his extra

Fig. 78

Fig. 77

pawn on the queen's side because it is doubled, e.g. 1. ... c5 2. c4 c6 3. f4 b5 4. b3!–and not 4. c x b5? c x b5 allowing Black a candidate. A healthy majority versus a crippled majority can weigh heavily in the endgame. (Note this additional weakness of the doubled pawn.)

Before we move on to discuss planning, let us look at an endgame which illustrates several important points:
a) An outside passed pawn is a passed pawn at the edge of the board. It is especially valuable in the endgame because it will either be too far away to be captured or it will cause the opponent to decentralise his pieces in order to capture it.
b) When advancing a healthy majority to create a passed pawn, the candidate should be advanced first.
c) Passed pawns should always be blockaded if possible.

In Figure 78 Black decides to chase White's outside passed 'a' pawn.
1. Ke3 Kb4 2. K x e4 Ka3 3. Kd4! K x a2 4. Kc3!

Blockading the black 'c' pawn from a distance is more effective than trying to capture it here, since Black's decentralised king is now cut off from the king's side and

White's candidate, the 'f' pawn, will be forced home. Had White tried 3. Kd5 K x a2 4. Kc6 Kb3! 5. K x c7 Kc4 Black would have had more chances of saving the game with his king in play. Now it is completely blocked, e.g. 4. ... Ka3 5. f4 Ka4 6. Kc4!, etc. or as in the game–4. ... Kb1 5. f4!

And not 5. g4? g5!, leaving White's candidate (the 'f' pawn) backward and his majority crippled. Advance the candidate first!
5. ... Kc1 6. g4 Kd1 7. f5! h6 8. h4 Ke2 9. g5

Black resigned: 9. ... Kf3 10. f6 and White will win easily.

Planning
'Better a bad plan than no plan at all' –the chessplayers' motto.

Opportunism at the chessboard will never succeed against an opponent who is proceeding in accordance with a plan. Tactical foresight and an understanding of general principles will help you to make individual moves, but positive play in chess means choosing the overall course a game is going to take. The ability to formulate plans in a comparatively quiet position is at least as important as the ability to calculate tricky variations.

Planning is very difficult, and you will need experience of playing chess before your plans really start to click. Here is an example of a game that required a series of concrete plans to win it; we join the game shown in Figure 79 after Black's thirteenth move.

White has a certain amount of pressure in the centre against Black's backward 'd' pawn, and a space advantage on the queen's side. He decides to expand further on this wing and to try and gain more control over the d5 square.
1. b4! b6

Fig. 79

White threatened 2. b5 Be8 3. B x f6 B x f6 4. Nd5 Qc5 5. N x f6 ch. g x f6 6. Nh4 with an attack, so Black prepares a retreat for his bishop along the c6–a8 diagonal to enable the capture of the white knight with his bishop after Nd5. However, the move played weakens Black's control over the c6 square and White finds a plan to exploit this:

a) To play Nd5 and, after B x d5 by Black, to recapture with the 'c' pawn.

b) To play B x f6, eliminating Black's last defender of the white squares.

c) Then to play b5 followed by Rc6 if possible.

2. Nd5! B x d5

Not 2. ... N x d5? 3. c x d5 and Black's bishop on c6 is lost because of the pin.

3. c x d5 Qb7 4. B x f6! B x f6 5. b5! Rc5! See Figure 80.

Preventing White's intended Rc6, but White did in fact expect this. He now chose the new plan:

a) To exchange rooks, allowing Black a protected passed pawn but creating the superb blockading square c4 for his knight.

b) To maneouvre his knight via d2 to c4.

c) If Black recaptures the rook with his 'd' pawn, to prepare the advance a4–a5 x b6 and subsequently to penetrate the enemy

position via the a-file.

d) If Black recaptures the rook with his 'b' pawn, to prepare the advance a4–a5 and b6 creating a dangerous passed pawn.

In fact there followed:

6. R x c5! b x c5 7. Rb1 Qb6 8. Nd2! Qa5 9. Qc2!

Denying access to the black queen.

9. ... Rb8 10. Nc4 Qc7 See Figure 81.

All as planned; Black can only defend in a painfully constricted position.

11. a4 Bd8 12. a5 Qd7 13. b6 a6 See Figure 82.

Another turning point. White had

Fig. 81

Fig. 82

expected 13. ... a x b6 14. a x b6, when he intended to make further inroads via the a-file. Black allows him a protected passed pawn, however, (protected in this context means by a pawn) in an effort to close the position. So a new plan is called for.

White decides to exploit the superior mobility of his pieces, which is due to the fact that Black is tied to defence of the 'd' pawn and obliged to block the 'b' pawn, in the following manner:

a) To play Ra1 and Qa4, exchanging Black's only potentially active piece, his queen, which might otherwise be used to

Fig. 80

39

create diversions by . . . Qg4 or . . . Qa4 if permitted.

b) To swing the rook across to the king's side via the third rank, in conjunction with pawn moves to open lines for the decisive penetration of this virtual extra piece.

14. Ra1! Kf8 15. Qa4! Q x a4 16. R x a4
Phase one completed.

16. . . . Ke7 17. Ra3! Rb7 18. h4 h5 19. Rf3! See Figure 83.

A thematic alternative was 19. g4! h x g4 20. Rg3 and the rook penetrates, but White allows himself the luxury of a tactical threat: 20. R x f7 ch! K x f7 21. N x d6 ch.

Fig. 83

and 22. N x b7. Black fails to find a sufficient defence:

19. . . . Rd7 20. b7! R x b7
Or 20. . . . Bc7 21. Nb6! Rd8 22. Nc8 ch. Ke8 23. Rb3 Bb8 24. Rb6 and White must win.

21. R x f7 ch! K x f7 22. N x d6 ch. Ke7 23. N x b7 Bc7 24. N x c5
And Black resigned: 24. . . . B x a5 25. N x a6 leaves him with a hopeless endgame two pawns down.

You will not always have positions where plans can be made and carried out as logically and consistently as in the above game, but you should always try to make some sort of plan. The tactical finish of the game was only made possible by the previous planned play: the pawn at b6, the knight at c4, and the rook at f3 did not get there by accident!

NOTE: This is the most difficult chapter in the book, and it will be some time before you master all it contains. It will repay you to study this section again after you have played some games, and if you record your moves you will be able to re-examine them in the light of these ideas, the accumulated wisdom of a hundred years.

Chapter Four
The Phases of the Game

Chess games are traditionally divided into three phases: the opening, the middlegame, and the endgame. The opening phase sees both sides aiming to develop their pieces and secure a fair share of the centre; in most cases, both sides will hurry to castle before the real struggles begin.

In the middlegame the two armies will be in contact, and, with a large number of pieces and choices of plan, this is perhaps the richest and most difficult phase of the game. The techniques appropriate to middlegame play have been discussed already in chapters Two and Three, and so will not be enlarged upon here.

The endgame can also be very complex and fascinating, despite the fact that most of the pieces have disappeared, and the struggle usually turns on the attempts of one or both players to queen their pawns. Despite the comparative tranquillity of endgames, precision is often vital in the timing of pawn advances, checks, and so on; many fine combinations have been dedicated to the theme of pawn promotion in the endgame.

In this chapter we shall examine some openings and endgames that you might encounter.

The Opening
As chess is a game of ever-increasing popularity, a large number of opening paths have been analysed and named. When you are beginning to play, however, it will not help you to memorise these openings in detail; your opponents will probably deviate from them, and you will do much better to understand the principles underlying opening play.

Therefore you should *not* just try to copy the moves given in the opening examples that follow every time you play a game. These examples are designed to help you understand opening principles, and represent but a very few of the enormous number of opening variations known and used today.

The Giuoco Piano Opening
1. e4 e5 2. Nf3 Nc6 3. Bc4 Bc5 4. Nc3 Nf6 5. 0–0 0–0 6. d3 d6 See Figure 84.

This opening illustrates a method by which both sides develop safely and effectively, with a share in the centre. It is a very old opening, little played today because of the comparatively tame positions that tend to arise.

Incidentally, do not copy your opponent's moves for too long in a symmetrical opening! Here, after 7. Bg5 Bg4 8. h3 h6? Black loses a pawn: 9. h x g4 h x g5 10. N x g5 and White's queen protects his 'g' pawn.

The Ruy Lopez Opening
1. e4 e5 2. Nf3 Nc6 3. Bb5 a6 See Figure 85.

Another very old opening, named after a Spanish cleric. Black's third move demonstrates that the White 'threat' of 4. B x c6 and 5. N x e5 is only apparent, e.g. 4. B x c6 d x c6! 5. N x e5? Qd4 6. Nf3 Q x e4 ch. assures Black a completely satisfactory

Fig. 84   41

game; all his pieces can be developed quite easily, and White will lose the castling privilege after 7. Kf1 or 7. Qe2 Q x e2 ch. 8. K x e2, etc.

This illustrates the rule: do not waste too much time hunting pawns in the opening!

Continuations from Figure 85 can take two forms, and both are still seen quite often today.

a) 4. Ba4 Nf6 5. 0–0 Be7
After 5. . . . N x e4 6. d4! White has good chances of attacking in the centre.
6. Re1 b5 7. Bb3 d6 8. c3
Preparing d4! with a strong centre.

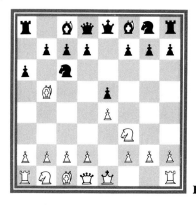

Fig. 85

8. . . . 0–0 9. h3
If 9. d4 Bg4!, pinning the knight, fights for control of d4 and e5.
9. . . . Na5 10. Bc2 c5 11. d4 Qc7 See Figure 86.

A difficult struggle lies ahead, with White's chances mainly on the king's side and Black's on the queen's side.

b) 4. B x c6 d x c6 5. 0–0 See Figure 87.
In this position Black's doubled pawn is considered to be offset by his possession of the two bishops. White would like to play d4 and exchange his 'd' pawn for Black's 'e' pawn to obtain the pawn structure of Figure

Fig. 87

77, which gives him good winning chances should an endgame arise; Black seeks a complicated position and open lines for his bishops.

Just in case you should happen to play this opening, beware the trap 5. . . . Bg4 6. h3 h5! 7. h x g4? h x g4 8. N x e5 Qh4 and Black forces mate. Best is 7. d3.

The King's Gambit
1. e4 e5 2. f4!?
The symbol !? means an interesting move. The objects of this pawn offer are: a) to decoy Black's pawn allowing White to establish a strong classical centre with a later d4, and b) to recapture the 'f' pawn later with play down the f-file.
2. . . . e x f4 3. Nf3
Better than the immediate 3. d4, which is met by the awkward reply 3. . . . Qh4 ch! See Figure 88.

Now there are two different attitudes towards the follow-up, illustrated by these lines:
a) 3. . . . d6 4. d4 g5 5. Bc4 g4!?
Hoping to drive White's knight away, allowing Black his queen check at h4.
6. 0–0!? g x f3 7. Q x f3 See Figure 89. Black has spent six pawn moves gaining

Fig. 86

Fig. 88

Fig. 89

material, while White hopes to have built up enough development to conduct a strong attack. This is a very dangerous policy for the second player—do not make too many pawn moves in the opening!

b) 3. ... d5! 4. e x d5 Nf6 g. d4 Bd6 6. Bd3 0-0 See Figure 90.

Black has returned the gambit pawn for a lead in development. He will obtain adequate counterplay down the e-file, combined with an annoying pin by ... Bg4.

This is a modern approach to openings such as the King's Gambit—return the gambit pawn in order to seize the initiative

Fig. 90

with active piece play!

The Sicilian Defence
1. e4 c5

The Sicilian defence, typified by the above moves, is very popular with modern chess players, because it gives rise to a complex, unbalanced struggle. One line follows the path:

2. Nf3 d6 3. d4 c x d4 4. N x d4
Not 4. Q x d4? Nc6 and the queen must move again, illustrating the rules:
a) Do not waste time moving the same piece in the opening.

b) Do not bring out the queen too early (because she will be attacked and obliged to move again).
c) Develop with gain of time if possible.
4. ... Nc6 5. Nc3 Nf6

In Figure 91 White has an enduring space advantage in the centre. If Black reacts with a later ... e5, he will have to contend with a backward 'd' pawn, and White usually has too many pieces controlling d5 for Black to advance his 'd' pawn at an early stage.

Nevertheless, Black has a satisfactory scheme of development with the moves e6, Be7, Bd7, a6, Qc7 and 0-0. When he has

Fig. 91

completed these moves, he will set about expanding on the queen's side with ... b5, or in the centre with ... d5.

Incidentally, Black should not exchange 5. ... N x d4 6. Q x d4 because White's queen will then be strongly posted in the centre as she cannot be satisfactorily driven away for some time. Don't develop your opponent's pieces by exchanging.

From Figure 91 play might continue: 6. Bg5 e6 7. f4 Be7 8. Qd2 0-0 9. 0-0-0 a6 See Figure 92.

An exciting battle is in prospect. White will attack on the king's side and Black will

Fig. 92   43

counterattack by b5–b4 with a difficult struggle in which both kings come under fire.

The Queen's Gambit

1. d4 d5 2. c4! e6

This gambit may be accepted, e.g., 2. ... d x c4 3. e3 and White regains the pawn: 3. ... b5 4. a4! c6 (4. ... a6 5. a x b5 a x b5? 6. R x a8) 5. b3! c x b3 6. a x b5 c x b5 7. B x b5 ch. and 8. Q x b3. It is more usual, however, to decline the Queen's Gambit.

3. Nc3 Nf6 4. Bg5 Be7 See Figure 93.

Fig. 93

Black may prefer 4. ... Nbd7, which involves a trap: 4. ... Nbd7 5. c x d5 e x d5 6. N x d5? N x d5! (the 'relative pin' is broken) 7. B x d8 Bd4 ch. and White must interpose his queen: 8. Qd2 B x d2 ch. 9. K x d2 K x d8 and Black finishes a piece up.

In Figure 93 White has a slight advantage in development, due to the fact that his queen's bishop is developed outside his pawns, whereas Black's queen's bishop is harder to develop.

Many lines of the Queen's Gambit are known, and one of the easiest goes:

Fig. 94

5. e3 Nbd7 6. c x d5 e x d5 7. Bd3 0–0 8. Qc2 c6 9. Nf3 Re8

In Figure 94 both sides have nearly completed their development and the time is ripe to find a plan for the middlegame. The usual plans adopted are, for White, to prepare the advance b4–b5 attacking the base of Black's pawn chain; for Black, either to reciprocate by f4–f5 or to seek active piece play on the king's side.

You should always start making plans as soon as the critical features of the coming middlegame (e.g., pawn structure, available lines) have begun to show themselves.

The Benoni Defence

1. d4 Nf6 2. c4 c5!? 3. d5 See Figure 95.

A typical hypermodern opening (see Chapter Three). Black attends to the centre by means of a flanking blow rather than by direct occupation: if 3. d x c5, Qa5 ch. regains the pawn. Meanwhile, Black is planning to develop his king's bishop at g7 and tries to control the central squares e5 and d4 from a distance.

Play from Figure 95 may take several forms, e.g.:

a) 3. ... g6 4. Nc3 Bg7 5. e4 d6 6.

Fig. 95

Nf3 0–0 7. Be2 e6! 8. 0–0

The alternative 8. d x e6 B x e6 saddles Black with a backward 'd' pawn, it is true, but allows his knight to develop at c6 with immediate access to the squares d4 and e5. White players usually avoid this.

8. ... e x d5 9. c x d5 Re8 See Figure 96.

Black has pressure down the e-file and along the a1–h8 diagonal. White will defend his 'e' pawn and transfer his knight via d2 to c4, following up if he can with f4 and e5, attacking the base of Black's pawn chain and overrunning the centre. Black will try to restrain this and aim at b5 and a

Fig. 96

mobilisation of his queen's-side majority. Again, an unbalanced and difficult struggle.
b) 3. .... b5!? 4. c x b5 a6 5. b x a6 B x a6 6. Nc3 g6 7. e4 B x f1 8. K x f1 Bg7 9. g3 0–0 10. Kg2 d6 See Figure 97.

This variation is known as the *Volga Gambit*. Black has sacrificed a pawn for rapid development and will develop pressure with his queen and rooks down the a- and b-files, combined with his bishop acting on the long diagonal. An interesting battle of piece activity versus material will ensue.

In this small selection of openings you have seen a wide range of ideas and concrete possibilities. The main points to remember, however, are common to all good openings:
a) Always attend to the centre.
b) Develop rapidly and economically.
c) Do not waste time on premature raids.
d) Start planning as soon as the pawn structure is clarified.

The Endgame
Some aspects of endgame play have already been discussed in the previous two chapters, such as the necessity for centralisation (especially of the king), maintenance of

Fig. 97

active piece play, the importance of passed pawns and, especially, of outside passed pawns (see Figure 78). A further important element of endgames is technique; this means the ability to conduct certain recurring, simple endgames properly and efficiently. What follows is a selection of elementary techniques which you should master.

You should enlist the help of a friend to practise some of these set pieces; such practice will both save your time and help you to see the powers of the pieces in their clearest form.

The Elementary Mates
When one side has a bare king and the other, a king and piece or pieces, mate can usually be forced fairly simply by the following routine:
a) Bring your king up to the opposing king.
b) Drive the opposing king into the side or into a corner by cutting off its flight squares, after which mate follows quite quickly. Here are some examples.

K + Q v K
In Figure 98, White plays 1. Ke4! Kd6 2. Qc8!–better than 2. Qf6 ch? Kc5, when

Fig. 98

Black is no closer to the edge of the board.
Checks are not important at this stage; what is important is to cut off the squares available to the enemy king and drive it backwards.
After 2. Qc8! Ke7 is forced, and then comes 3. Ke5!–not 3. Kd5? Kf6!, or 3. Kf5 Kd6!, when again Black is wriggling away.
3. ... Kf7 4. Kf5
Not 4. Qd7 ch? Kg6
4. ... Ke7 5. Qc7 ch. Kf8 6. Kf6 and mate next move, e.g. 6... Ke8 7. Qe7 mate or 6. ... Kg8 7. Qg7 mate.

K + R v K

This is also quite easy, as long as you remember not to bother about checks but concentrate on encirclement. In Figure 99, White plays:

1. Ke4! Kd6 2. Rc2! Ke6 3. Rc6 ch. Kd7 4. Kd5 Ke7 5. Rd6!, not 5. Rc7 ch? Kf6!

5. ... Kf7 6. Re6! Kg7 7. Ke5! Kf7 8. Kf5! Kg7 9. Re7 ch! and now:

a) 9. ... Kh6 10. Ra7! (*zugzwang*) 10. ... Kh7 11. Rh7 mate.

b) 9. ... Kf8 10. Kf6 Kg8 11. Ra7 Kh8 12. Kg6 Kg8 13. Ra8 mate.

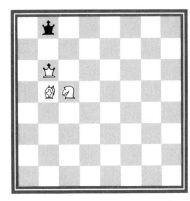

Fig. 101

K + B + N v K

This mate is far harder than the others we have looked at, and can only be forced when the king is trapped in a corner where the bishop controls the corner square, as in Figure 101:

1. Bd7 Ka8 2. Bh3 Kb8 3. Na6 ch. Ka8 4. Bg2 mate.

Although it is difficult to force the king into the correct corner, the same restriction technique applies (using the knight to cover squares of the colour the bishop does not control). You should practise this mate carefully, starting with the pieces anywhere, until you feel you have mastered it.

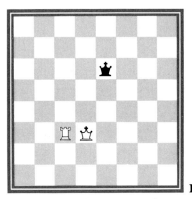

Fig. 99

K + 2 Bs v K

Again, quite easy – force the king into a corner. Here is one line from the Figure 100 position:

1. Ke4! Kd6 2. Bd4 Kc6 3. Ba4 ch. Kd6 4. Bb6! Ke6 5. Bc5! Kf6 6. Bd7! Kg5 7. Be7 ch. Kg6 8. Be8 ch. Kg7 9. Kf5 Kh6 10. Kf6 Kh7 11. Bg6 ch. Kh8

– or 11. ... Kh6? 12. Bf8 mate.

12. Bc2

and not 12. Kf7? stalemate.

12. ... Kg8 13. Kg6 Kh8 14. Bbl! Kg8 15. Ba2 ch. Kh8 16. Bf6 mate.

K + 2Ns v K

Mate cannot be forced with two knights although the mating position of Figure 102 is possible.

Why isn't this mate forced? An extrapolation backwards from Figure 102 will soon show us. The last two moves must have been 1. Ng5 ch. Kh8 2. Ng6 mate. However, Black would have been able to play 1. ... Kh6!, since wherever White's second knight (the one at g6) came from, it must have started on a black square and therefore it could not have been controlling

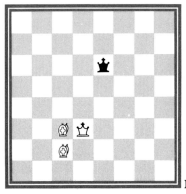

Fig. 100

Fig. 102

h6, which is also black.

This is a weakness of the knight in the endgame; it can only move from squares of one colour to squares of the opposite colour, and is thus a somewhat clumsy piece.

As you will already have discovered if you tried the exercise suggested in Chapter One, K + B or K + N is insufficient material to mate. With more material than in the examples above, mate is very easy.

One point to emphasise is that you should beware of stalemating the opposing king while you are chasing it into the corner!

Pawn Endings

In endings where one side has K + P v K, or K + piece + P v K + piece, the key to success is control of the squares between the pawn and the queening square.

K + P v K

In Figure 103, *zugzwang* is the vital factor. If it is White to move, the position is drawn: White must play either, for example, 1. Kb6 K x d7 or 1. Kd6 stalemate.

If Black is to move, however, he loses. His only move is 1. . . . Ke7 when 2. Kc7 forces the pawn home.

Fig. 103

It transpires that the only way in which a winning position can be forced is for White to have his king in front of the pawn before it reaches the fifth rank. To verify this let us look at two possible lines of play from Figure 104.

a) 1. d4? Kd7 2. Kd2 Kd6 3. Kd3 Kd5 4. Kc3 Kd6!

The defence should always keep the king on the 'reserve blockading square' if possible.

5. Kc4 Kc6!
–but not 5. . . . Kd7 6. Kd5!
6. d5 ch. Kd6 7. Kd4 Kd7! 8. Ke5

Fig. 104

Ke7! 9. d6 ch. Kd7 10. Kd5 Kd8! 11. Kc6 Kc8! 12. d7 ch. Kd8
And we reach Figure 103 with White's turn to move–draw.

b) 1. Ke2! Kd7 2. Kd3! Kd6 3. Kd4! Ke6 4. Kc5! Kd7–or 4. . . . Ke5 5. d4 ch. Ke6 6. Kc6 Ke7 7. d5 Kd8 8. Kd6 reaching the main line again.
5. Kd5!
And not 5. d4? Kc7! when either 6. d5 Kd7, etc. or 6. Kd5 Kd7 7. Ke5 Ke7 8. Kd5 Kd7, etc., draws.
5. . . . Ke7 6. Kc6 Ke6 7. d4 Ke7 8. d5 Kd8 9. Kd6! meeting 9. . . . Ke8 with 10. Kc7, or 9. . . . Kc8 with 10. Ke7, followed by queening the 'd' pawn.

The side with the extra pawn should always try to face the opposing king directly with the opponent to move (as at the end of line b), whereupon the opponent will be forced to step aside.

An ending with a rook's pawn is always drawn if the opposing king can reach the bishop's square closest to the rook's pawn in time. Here are three ways in which the position shown in Figure 105 may end in a draw.
a) 1. a5 Kd6 2. a6 Kc6 3. a7 Kb7 draw.
b) 1. Kc5 Kd7 2. Kb6 Kc8 and now:

Fig. 105 47

3. a5 Kb8 4. a6 Ka8 5. a7 stalemate.
3. Ka7 Kc7! 4. a5 Kc8! 5. a6 Kc7 6.
Ka8 Kc8 7. a7 Kc7 stalemate.

K + minor piece + P v K + minor piece
This is almost invariably a draw if the
defending king is nearby, since the piece can
be sacrificed for the pawn to give a drawn
ending. The win can only be forced if the
defending king is elsewhere and the
attacking king and piece can be used to
prevent the other piece from sacrificing
itself for the pawn, as in Figure 106.
White plays 1. d7 2. Bc7 and 3. d8 = Q. If

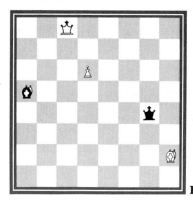

Fig. 106

Black's bishop stood at a4 instead of a5 a
draw would be inevitable, or if it stood at d2,
e.g., 1. d7 Bg5! and White cannot block the
bishop's control of d8.

There are also two cases where K + minor
piece + rook's pawn draw against a lone
king.

In Figure 107 White's bishop does not
control the queening square, a8. It is said to
be the wrong-colour bishop, and this ending
is met quite often. Black draws simply by
keeping his king on the squares a8 and b8
until White stalemates him in the
corner–you can confirm this for yourself.

Another, slightly less common case
appears in Figure 108.

Black draws by 1. . . . Kf7! and the white
king cannot escape; the black king just
moves from f7 to f8, and the knight cannot
prevent this, e.g. 2. Ne5 ch. Kf8 3. Nd7
ch. Kf7, etc.

This is another example of the
clumsiness of the knight: it cannot mark
time. Black cannot draw by 1. . . . Kf8? 2.
Ne5!, however; the king must go to the
square where it will be checked.

K + R + P v K + R
Figure 109 is called the Lucena position
after a player who first analysed it nearly 500
years ago.

White cannot win by 1. Rd1, intending 2.
Ke7, etc., because of 1. . . . Kf7. Nor is 1.
Ke7 any help, e.g., 1. . . . Re2 ch. 2.
Kd6 Rd2 ch. 3. Kc6 Rc2 ch. 4. Kb5
Rd2, etc.

The winning technique is called 'bridge
building'. White plays:
1. Rf4!
On 1. Rf5 Kg6 interferes.
1. . . . Rc1 2. Ke7 Re1 ch. 3. Kd6 Rd1
ch. 4. Ke6 Re1 ch.
Or 4. . . . Rd2 5. Rf5! followed by 6. Rd5

Fig. 108

Fig. 107

Fig. 109

48

ensures the promotion.

5. Kd5 Rd1 ch. 6. Rd4 and White wins.

Rook and pawn endings are very difficult to conduct despite the fact that they occur more frequently than any other. Whole books have been written on the subject! Many pretty finesses are available to both sides, and exact calculation is often called for. However, certain principles can be used which will help you in these endings. They are:

a) Always try to keep the rook active.

b) In general, rooks are best placed behind passed pawns (either your own or your opponent's).

c) With only one pawn, use your rook to cut off the king from the queening square—e.g., in Figure 109, Black's king cannot cross the f-file.

Queen endings

These are even more difficult than rook endings, since on an open board the queen can deliver check after check. With K + Q + P *v* K + Q the general rule for the attacking side is to bring the king as close as possible to the opposing king, hoping to answer a queen check by interposing your own queen with check and exchanging queens.

Such positions are too complex for discussion here; however, there are two cases where K + P can draw against K + Q which you should know about. These occur when the pawn is a rook's or bishop's pawn on the seventh rank, with the defending king close by and the attacking king far off.

In Figure 110 Black plays 1. ... Qb4 ch. 2. Ka8! and if Black advances his king it is stalemate. Black must either keep checking, in which case White's king oscillates between a8, b8 and b7, permit the pawn to queen, or permit stalemate.

In Figure 111 Black can try 1. ... Qb4 ch. 2. Ka8!

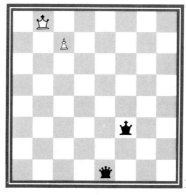
Fig. 111

Not 2. Kc8? giving Black time for 2. ... Ke4!, bringing his king closer. White maintains the threat of promoting.

2. ... Qa5 ch. 3. Kb8 Qb6 ch. 4. Ka8!

And White draws: on 4. ... Q x c7 it is stalemate, so again Black must keep checking.

These situations are only possible with a rook's pawn or a bishop's pawn because of the stalemate positions with the king in the corner. You should practise these positions. In the other cases, the side with the queen will be able to force the opposing king to block his own pawn's queening square, so allowing the friendly king to approach.

More Complex Endgames

A detailed discussion of more complex endgames is beyond the scope of this book, but if you wish to take chess seriously, study of endgames is essential. Some of the general principles underlying endgame play have been outlined at the beginning of this section and in the previous chapter, and you will find a selection of reference works on the endgame in the bibliography at the end of the book.

Some very fine players have felt that an understanding of endgames is essential to the understanding of the entire game of chess, since nowhere else does one see the full powers of the individual pieces so acutely displayed.

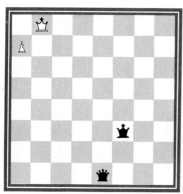
Fig. 110

Chapter Five
Some Illustrative Games

In this chapter we shall look at some sample games of chess, and try to tie in some of the things you have learned with a living chess situation. You might find it interesting to try to guess the next move each time you come across a figure to test yourself.

Game No. 1
An example showing how a local superiority in space, based on a strong centre, can lead to a powerful wing attack.
1. e4 Nf6   Figure 112.

This sophisticated and provocative move is known as Alekhine's Defence, after a

Fig. 112

former world champion who perfected it. Black provokes 2. e5, hoping that the further advance of White's pawn will lessen its command over the centre; some players have thought that Black's plan is too time consuming to be reliable.
2. e5 Nd5
3. Nc3!? N x c3
4. d x c3   Figure 113.

Now White has more space and faster development potential, offset by the slight weakening of his pawn structure due to the doubled 'c' pawns.
4. . . . d6

Fig. 113

5. Bc4!
Indirectly protecting the 'e' pawn. On 5. . . . d x e5? there would follow 6. B x f7 ch! K x f7 7. Q x d8 and White wins. So Black defends the f7 square.
5. . . . e6
6. Nf3   Figure 114.

White's development proceeds apace.
6. . . . Nc6
7. Bf4 Be7

Now both sides are ready for king's-side castling, but White would prefer to castle queen's side and develop an attack to exploit his superior development—see Chapter

Fig. 114

Three, 'When to Attack'.

8. Qe2! d5
9. 0–0–0! Figure 115.

So that if 9. . . . d x c4 10. R x d8 ch. wins Black's queen for rook and bishop–9 points for 8½, according to our scheme in Chapter One.

9. . . . Bd7
10. Bd3 f6?!

The sign ?! means a dubious move. Here Black seeks to challenge White's constricting pawn at e5, but it is too well guarded for this attack to have any effect. White now gains space on the king's side,

Fig. 115

setting a trap which his opponent falls into.
11. h4! 0–0? Figure 116.

Loses, but if 11. . . . f x e5 12. N x e5 Black's 'e' pawn is weak and backward.
12. B x h7 ch! K x h7
13. Ng5 ch! Figure 117.

The bishop sacrifice, removing pawn cover from the opposing king, is followed by a knight sacrifice designed to open the lines h1–h8 for White's rook and e2–h5 for White's queen.
13. . . . f x g5

Alternatives:
a) 13. . . . Kg6 14. h5 ch! and now either

Fig. 116

Fig. 117

14. . . . Kh6 15. Nf7 dble. ch. followed by 16. N x d8, winning Black's queen for two pieces, or 14. . . . Kf5 15. g4 ch! K x f4 16. Nh3 mate!
b) 13. . . . Kg8 14. Qh5! (threat Qh7 mate) 14. . . . f x g5 15. h x g5 and White wins, e.g. 15. . . . R x f4 16. Qh8 ch. Kf7 17. g6 ch! K x g6 18. Qh5 mate. Black's best try is 15. . . . B x g5 16. B x g5, when White still wins but less easily.

The reader should examine these variations carefully.
14. h x g5 dis. ch. Figure 118.
White has sacrificed two pieces, but mate

Fig. 118

is now forced.
14. . . . Kg8 Figure 119.

Or 14. . . . Kg6 15. Qh5 ch. Kf5 16. g6 dis. ch! K x f4 17. g3 ch. Ke4 18. Rhe1 mate.

Now on 15. Qh5, Black could transpose to the comparatively best defence of line (b) above (from Black's thirteenth move) with 15. . . . B x g5, but there is something better!
15. Rh8 ch! K x h8
If 15. . . . Kf7 16. Qh5 ch. g6 17. Rh7 ch. followed by 18. Q x g6 ch. mates quickly. The reader should confirm this.
16. Qh5 ch. Kg8

Fig. 119

Fig. 120

17. g6! Figure 120.

In this position mate is inevitable, so BLACK RESIGNED.

The threat is 18. Qh7 mate, and on 17. ... R x f4 comes 18. Qh7 ch. Kf8 19. Qh8 mate. Black's extra rook and three pieces are no help at all!

Game No. 2

Here we see a premature wing attack refuted by counterattack in the centre.
1. d4 g6
2. e4 c6
3. h4!? d5! Figure 121.

Fig. 121

White's decision to launch an immediate attack via h4–h5 x g6 is promptly met by retaliation in the centre!
4. e5
Trying to 'fix' the centre before continuing with his plan.
4. ... h5
5. Nh3! Figure 122.

Usually knights develop towards the centre, but here the knight is better off on h3 than f3 because from the former position it can reach f4 or g5–a concrete reason for a move is better than blind trust in general principles.

Fig. 122

5. ... Bf5
Playing the bishop outside the pawn chain before completing it with ... e6.
6. Bd3 Nh6
7. Ng5? Figure 123.

But now 7. Bg5! would have been stronger. This second knight move is premature and lacks point.
7. ... e6
8. B x f5 N x f5
9. c3 c5! Figure 124.

Black avoids the routine 9. ... Nd7, and instead commences immediate operations in the centre–his queen's knight will exert

Fig. 123

Fig. 124

more pressure from c6.

10. g4?

Pursuing the mirage of an attack, but now Black will develop with alarming speed due to his threats against d4. However, White already had problems with his queen's-side development, probably stemming from his mistake on the seventh move.

10. ... h x g4

11. Q x g4 Nc6 Figure 125.

12. Nf3

A sad retreat; however, if 12. Be3 Qb6! attacks two pawns, and on 12. d x c5 N x e5 the white centre disappears without trace.

Fig. 125

Fig. 126

12. ... Qb6!

13. d x c5 B x c5 Figure 126.

Black's development is complete, he is threatening 14. ... B x f2 ch., and he is ready to castle queen's side followed by an attack on the king's side himself, where White's premature pawn advances have left a wake of weaknesses.

14. Rh2 0-0-0

15. Nbd2 Qc7!

Winning a pawn by force.

16. Qf4 f6 Figure 127.

White's 'e' pawn is pinned, and must fall.

17. Nb3 f x e5

Fig. 127

18. Qg4 Figure 128.

Black now dominates the centre completely and White's uncastled king will soon become the target for a mopping-up operation.

18. ... Bd6

19. Rh3

Not 19. Q x g6? e4! 20. Q x e6 ch. Qd7 and Black threatens both the knight at f3 and the rook at h2.

19. ... e4!

20. Nfd4 Ne5 Figure 129.

Attacking the queen, defending the 'g' pawn, and eyeing the d3 and f3 squares.

Fig. 128 53

Fig. 129

Such is the power of a centralised knight!
21. Qg2 N x h4
22. R x h4
Desperation; White will regain the exchange, but his position is now beyond salvation.
22. ... R x h4
23. N x e6 Figure 130.
23. ... Qh7!
  Black prepares the coup-de-grâce by assuming control of the h-file–an amusing turnabout of White's intentions with his aggressive third and tenth moves.
24. N x d8 Rh1 ch. Figure 131.

Fig. 130

Fig. 131

Certainly not 24. ... K x d8? 25. Bg5 ch! Even won positions can be thrown away through a moment's carelessness.
25. Kd2
Or 25. Ke2 Qh5 ch. 26 Kd2 Qd1 ch. 27. Ke3 Nc4 mate.
25. ... Nf3 ch.
26. Kc2 Figure 132.
  And now if 26. Ke2 or 26. Ke3, Black has 26. ... Re1 mate!
26. ... Ne1 ch.
WHITE RESIGNED. His queen is lost.

Before we look at our third illustrative game,

Fig. 132

you should acquaint yourself with the descriptive system of notation. Widely used in English- and Spanish-speaking countries, it is less economical than the algebraic system (which you should have mastered by now), but you will need to know it in order to read a great number of books which still use it today.
  In this system, each player names the squares after his pieces and the distance from their bases, as in Figure 133.
  The pieces are symbolised, as in the algebraic notation, by R, N, B, Q, K, and the pawns by P (Kt is sometimes used for the Knight). The name of the piece is written first, followed by a dash, then the square the piece goes to, e.g., the move you know as 1. e4 is written 1. P–K4.
  The symbols QR, QN, QB, etc., stand for queen's rook, queen's knight, queen's bishop and so on. The names of the squares remain the same, of course, even after the pieces have moved.
  It is not always necessary to specify whether a piece is moving to a queen's-side square or a king's-side square, since there will not always be a choice of which R1, or which B4, etc., a piece can go to. However, KR1 or QB4 are used to guard against

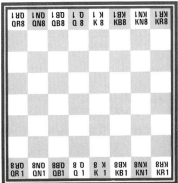

Fig. 133

Fig. 135

ambiguity when the same type of piece can move to either R1 or to either B4.

The descriptive system also uses the symbols 0–0 and 0–0–0 for castling, like the algebraic, the symbol x for a capture and the symbols !, ?, !? and ?! to annotate the moves.

Game No. 3 is written in descriptive notation, so you will have a chance to acquaint yourself with it.

Game No. 3

In this game we see exploitation of weakness over a complex of squares by

Fig. 134

means of a king's-side attack justified by a firm centre.

1. P–QB4   Figure 134.

A hypermodern opening; White controls his Q5 (d5) square from the sidelines. This is known as the English opening.

1. ... P–K4
2. N–QB3 N–KB3
3. P–K3 B–N5

Reaching the position of Figure 135; if you failed to follow this, you should go back and try again. Simply B–N5 suffices to describe Black's third move, since QN5 is the only N5 square available to a black bishop.

4. KN–K2 0–0
5. P–KN3?! R–K1   Figure 136.

White's fifth move invites a potential weakness on the white squares Q3, KB3 and KR3, but Black cannot exploit this at once. Instead he develops his rook, guarding his central pawn, and preparing a possible retreat for his KB to KB1.

6. B–N2 P–B3!

Intending to obtain a classical centre with P–Q4.

7. 0–0 P–Q4   Figure 137.

Black now has a very firm central hold and White must play vigorously to avoid being

Fig. 136

Fig. 137   55

overrun; he will experience difficulty developing his queen's bishop.

8. P x P   P x P
9. P–Q4   P–K5   Figure 138.

An important moment. The central situation has been clarified, and a middlegame plan must be evolved.

In Figure 138 White should try to gain play down the QB file, combined with attacks on the black QP. Black, on the other hand, would like to consolidate his centre and attempt to infiltrate White's king's side via his weakened white squares.

10. Q–N3!   N–B3

Fig. 138

11. N–B4!
Virtually forcing the following exchange, since 11. ... B–K3 invites the removal of his valuable attacking bishop.

11. ...   B x N   Figure 139.
12. Q x B
Or 12. P x B N–QR4! 13. Q–B2 N–B5 with a firm outpost in front of the backward QBP–a further white-square weakness which White rightly avoids.

12. ...   B–N5!
13. R–K1?!
Preparing a retreat square for his knight after Black's next move. However, a better

Fig. 139

way of doing so was by 13. Q–Q2!, since the rooks belong on the QB file. White's best plan was Q–Q2 followed by P–N3!, B–QR3! and swinging the rooks to the QB file.

13. ...   P–KN4   Figure 140.
Now Black makes visible progress.

14. N–K2   Q–Q2!
15. K–R1
Preparing N–N1 to defend his weak squares at KB3 and KR3.

15. ...   QR–QB1   Figure 141.
16. Q–Q2
Otherwise Black will discover an attack on

Fig. 140

Fig. 141

White's queen. Now Black controls the QB-file as well!

16. ...   Q–B4!
17. R–B1?
Inconsistent–better 17. N–N1 at once. This loss of time soon proves fatal.

17. ...   B–B6   Figure 142.
18. N–N1
On 18. B x B P x B 19. N–N1 (not 19. N–B3? Q–R6! 20. R–KN1 N–N5 followed by 21. ... Q x RP mate.) 19. ... N–K5 20. Q–Q1 P–N5 Black has a dominating centre and the white knight at N1 is immobilised forever.

Fig. 142

Fig. 144

Fig. 143

Fig. 145

18. ... R–K3!

Threat 19. ... N–KN5 and 20. ... R–R3 with a decisive attack.

19. P–KR3   Figure 143.

19. ... N–KN5!

Anyway! Now if 20. P x N   R–R3 ch.   21. N–R3   R x N ch.   22. K–N1   Q x P White is lost, e.g. 23. B x R   Q x B and 24. ... Q–N7 mate, or 23. B x B   P x B followed by 24. ... R–R8 ch.   25. K x R   Q–R6 ch.   26. K–N1   Q–N7 mate.

And if 20. B x B   P x B, 21. Q–Q1   R–R3! with the possibilities 22. Q x P   R x P ch! 23. K–N2 (or 23. N x R   Q x Q ch., etc.) 23. ... R–R7 mate!, or 22. N x P   N x KP! 23. P x N (or 23. B x N   Q x P ch. 24. K–N1   Q–R8 mate) 23. ... Q x P ch. 24.

K–N1   Q x P mate.

20. N x B   P x N

21. P x N   Figure 144.

21. ... Q x P

22. K–N1

White is quite helpless. On 22. B x P R–R3 ch. 23. K–N1   Q x B and 24. ... R–R8 mate, or 22. Q–Q1   R–R3 ch. 23. K–N1   Q–R4! 24. R–K1   Q–R7 ch. 25. K–B1   Q x B mate.

22. ... R–R3!

23. R–Q1   Q–R4!   Figure 145.

And mate is inevitable, so WHITE RESIGNED. On 24. B x P   Q x B followed by 25. ... R–R8 mate, and on 24. K–B1 Q–R8 ch! 25. B x Q   R x B mate. A fine exploitation of white-square weakness.

Further Reading

There are several good chess magazines: The *British Chess Magazine* and *Chess* are both published in the U.K., and there is the American *Chess Review*. For the new player, the very practical chess pages of *Games & Puzzles* magazine (available in both the U.K. and the U.S.) are excellent.

The game has a huge literature, and the following is a necessarily brief selection of good books that are available.

Tactics

The Chess Sacrifice by V. Vukovic (G. Bell, 1968). This is regarded as a classic on the subject.
The Penguin Book of Chess Positions by C. H. O'D. Alexander (Penguin, 1973). A little paperback which goes far in instruction and entertainment.

Strategy

My System by A. Nimzovich (G. Bell, 1929). The hypermodern chessplayer's bible, and well worth the difficulty of reading.
Judgement and Planning in Chess by M.

Euwe (G. Bell, 1953). A clear and helpful guide.

Openings

The Ideas behind the Chess Openings by R. Fine (G. Bell, 1943). At this stage of your chess thinking, this work will be of more use to you than the many specialised books available on specific openings.

The Endgame

Basic Chess Endings by R. Fine (G. Bell, 1941). A very dry, technical but complete reference book. You may find this heavy going but it is very good.

Game Collections

There are a large number of books available in which a selection of annotated games by strong grandmasters, often world champions, are the theme. These books are perhaps the most enjoyable, instructive and painless way of studying the game. A selection should be available in your local library.

Index

Alekhine's Defence 50
Algebraic notation 10, 15
Attacking 32

Benoni Defence opening
  44–45
Bishops, endgame
  techniques 46
  movements of the 12
  strategy 28
Bridge building 48

Capturing 11
Centralisation 29–31
  classical centre 29, 42
  hypermodern strategy
  30, 44
Check 14
  discovered 18
  double 18
  perpetual 14–15, 22
Checkmate 14

Decoy combinations 18–20
  line-clearing decoy 20
  overloaded pieces 19
  smothered mate decoy
  19–20
  tempo-gaining decoy 20
  undermining
  combinations 19
Descriptive notation 10,
  54–55
Desperado 23
Draws 14–15

En passant rule 11–12
En prise 17
Endgame, strategy 37, 38,
  41
  technique 45–49
English opening 55
Exchanging 32, 43

Fifty move rule 14
Fool's mate 15
Forks 17

Giuoco Piano opening 41

Initial position 9

King, castling 13–14
  movements of the 13
King's Gambit opening
  42–43
Knights, endgame
  techniques 46–47
  movements of the 12–13
  strategy 31–32

Legal moves 14
Legal's Mate 21
Lucena position 48

Middlegame, the 41

Opening moves 41–45
Origins of chess 9

Pawns, backward 33, 35
  candidates 37–38
  chains 35, 36
  doubled 34, 38
  endgame techniques
  47–49
  isolated 33, 35
  majorities 38
  movements of the 11
  passed 34, 37, 38
  pawns and the king
  36–37
  promotion 11, 21, 41
  strategy 32–38
  weak squares 35–36
Philidor 32
Philidor's Legacy 20

Pins 18
Planning 38–40

Queen, endgame
    techniques 45–46, 49
  movements of the 13
Queen's Gambit opening
  44

Resignation 14
Rooks, endgame
    techniques 46, 48–49
  movements of the 12
  strategy 27
Ruy Lopez opening 41–42

Scholar's mate 15–16
Sicilian Defence opening
  43–44
Skewers 17
Stalemate 15
Steinitz, William 32
Strengths of the pieces 15

Threefold repetition 14
Touch-and-move 14

Volga Gambit 45

Zugzwang 22–23, 47
Zwischenzug 23, 27, 30